Free Yourself

from

Chronic Fatigue

and

Fibromyalgia:

A Journey to Recovery

by

Dr. Patty Butts, PhD, LPC

Mill Creek Press
Salt Lake City, Utah

Published in the United States by Mill Creek Press.

MILL CREEK PRESS is a registered trademark of
Mill Creek Press, LLC

Library of Congress Control Number:: 2008921629

ISBN: 978-0-9798187-0-7

Printed in the United States of America on acid-free paper

pfb32975
First Edition

Cover Design by Bill Witsberger

This book is dedicated to all those who struggle with debilitating illness and have hope for recovery.

TABLE OF CONTENTS

1.   **From the Belly of the Whale**.................................... 1
My Journey to Recovery from Chronic Fatigue and Fibromyalgia

2.   **Candida-A Major Player in CFIDS and Fibromyalgia...** 15
Rodger Murphee, author of *Treating and Beating Fibromyalgia and Chronic Fatigue,* says studies have shown that up to 90% of FMS/CFIDS patients have a yeast overgrowth.

3.   **pH Balance in the Body**.................................... 23
According to Dr. Robert Young, over-acidification of body fluids and tissues underlies almost all disease. If tissue pH deviates too far to the acid side, oxygen levels decrease and cellular metabolism will stop.

4.   ***The China Study*-Dangers of Meat and Dairy**............. 31
The China Study, by Dr. T. Colin Campbell is the largest and most comprehensive study ever done on diet, disease and nutrition. Findings indicate that autoimmune diseases, heart disease, cancer, diabetes and other degenerative diseases can be reversed by diet.

5.   **Diet to Eliminate Yeast and Build Immune System...** 35
The body can only function normally when the reaction of fluids is balanced so a correct choice of foods that include 80% alkaline vegetables, fruits or foods is essential to maintain the proper pH for optimal health.

6.   **Results of an Alkaline Diet**.................................... 45
Results of an alkaline diet on patients with CFIDS/FMS who all experienced significant improvement in decreased muscle and joint pain. A hundred percent had improvement in 13 out of 16 symptoms.

7.   **Supplements for Treating Yeast, Enhancing Immune System**.. 51
Supplements that may be helpful in eliminating yeast overgrowth and enhancing immune response..

8.   Irritable Bowel Syndrome.. **59**
According to Dr. Jacob Teitelbaum, "Most people who have irritable bowel syndrome, or 'spastic colon', have yeast overgrowth or parasites." He goes on to say, "The best marker I have found for recurrent yeast overgrowth (candida) is a return of bowel symptoms, with gas, bloating, diarrhea, or constipation."

9.   Pain Management.. **63**
Every red blood cell in our bodies is composed of the foods we eat. The more acidic-the more lactic acid in our body, the more pain we will experience. Diet, supplements, lymphasizing, massage, movement, a mini trampoline, accupunture, attitude, and self hypnosis can help alleviate pain.

10.   Professional Help and Resources **73**
Resources for support groups, alternative and medical help.

11.   Overcoming Depression & the Blues..................... **79**
Symptoms and causes of depression. Activities to overcome Depression

12.   Healing from the Heart.. **87**
Emotions have as much to do with the body as they do the brain. "Freeze Frame," technique can change negative neural pathways, help you heal and become more optimistic and hopeful.

13.   Optimism-How to Get it and Keep it..................... **91**
When you can't change your situation you can change your attitude and internal self talk. You can learn to be an optimist rather than a pessimist. We are not born winners or losers, we are born choosers. We are responsible for our own happiness. No one else can make us happy.

14.   Win-Win Communication -Taking Back Your Power.. 97
Assertive behavior is the ability to honestly express your feelings, rights, opinions, thoughts, and beliefs in a direct way without trampling on the rights of others. An assertive person is able to deal effectively with others and can communicate expectations without humiliating, dominating, or degrading the other person.

**15.   Deep Relaxation/Self Hypnosis for Relaxation &
Healing**.. **103**

If there is built up tension in your body, it's almost impossible to deeply relax, but these simple steps can relieve stress and promote healing.

16.   Humor as a Healing Tool...................................... **105**

Laughter reduces the level of stress hormones like cortisol, adrenaline, epinephrine and growth hormone. Through humor, you can soften some of the worst blows that life delivers. Once you find laughter, you can survive even the most painful situations.

17.   Affirmations for Health.. **113**

How we think determines how we feel, and how we feel often determines our actions. By developing positive self-talk, we can conquer our negative feelings

17.   Fears-Facing Fears... **117**

We should fear some things-drinking poisons, leaping off tall buildings, and situations in which our physical body is in danger of extinction. "All other fears-the ones we face each day--are illusions. Fear is your negative self talk that you can conquer.

19.   Insomnia and Circadian Rhythms........................ **121**

When working properly, our bodies respond to nature's cues to create their ideal rhythms. For example, the human circadian rhythm will respond to the morning light of a new day, and again as the sun goes down by secreting the appropriate hormones and neurotransmitters. Possible solutions are given for balancing rhythms that are out of sync and also for eliminating insomnia.

20.   Recipes & the Shopping List................................ **133**

References.. **153**

Index.. **157**

Free Yourself

from

Chronic Fatigue

and

Fibromyalgia:

A Journey to Recovery

Chapter 1

FROM THE BELLY OF THE WHALE

"Chronic Fatigue is not death, but it takes your life away."

My Journey to Recovery from Chronic Fatigue and FMS

*A*fter a whirlwind courtship, I married a teacher at the school where I was a counselor. Having been nominated as one of the top counselors in our large school district and experiencing great rapport with the teenagers I worked with, I wasn't concerned about putting our five teenagers together. That was my first mistake. Little had I anticipated the chaos we would encounter. Blending five teenagers from two different families under one roof is not a move I'd recommend to anyone who wants to keep their sanity. I considered writing a book,

Cinderella from the Stepmother's Point of View, but didn't have the energy.

On what was to be a romantic vacation trip to Washington, D.C. with my husband, a tremendous fatigue engulfed my body. After walking less than ten yards, I had to sit down and rest. I would walk a few more steps and need to stop again. At the foot of the Washington Monument, I collapsed on the lawn and longed to be back home in bed. My body ached, my throat was sore, I felt dizzy and my thinking was confused. The stench of gas fumes and the unbearable humidity nauseated me beyond words.

Several weeks prior to the trip I had not been feeling well and had gone on a diet from the book, *Fit for Life*. I ate only fresh fruit in the morning and in the afternoon and evening resumed a fairly normal diet. Little did I know I had candida and that the sugary fruit was feeding my illness as fuel flames a fire. I thought I had a terrible case of the flu.

A stressful job, "Type A" personality, a chaotic and difficult family life, anemic, in need of a hysterectomy, experiencing insomnia, and an overly acidic body all contributed to the collapse of my health. I felt like a walking corpse. Trying to walk or get out of bed in the morning was like trying to resurrect the dead.

My feet felt like I was walking on pins and needles. The pain was excruciating, not only in my feet, but every joint and muscle. My lymph nodes ached and were swollen. My kidneys, liver and spleen hurt.

My doctor did a round of blood tests and found them nearly normal. I felt like I was dying yet he found nothing wrong. The doctor prescribed an anti-depressant that caused tardis dyskinesia (swelling of the tongue because of an allergic reaction to medication). My tongue became so thick that I couldn't enunciate my words properly. My mouth was constantly dry. When I tried to sleep, I felt like I was doing round after round of backward somersaults. My life was out of control. There were times I thought I might die if I didn't keep fighting to get well and just stayed in bed.

The doctor then referred me to a counselor who recommended Prozac as the panacea for everything. By the first week on this medication I was more depressed than ever. By the second week I felt suicidal. The counselor recommended doubling the dosage. No way was I going to double the dose and take the chance I'd feel twice as bad. I had done some research and found I was not the only one who had this response to Prozac. My life was so out of control I thought I might die and knew I could if I stopped fighting to get well and just stayed in bed.

Some of my friends and family thought I must be faking my illness because I looked perfectly fine. Others knew me to be hard working and dedicated and knew I must be ill.

I may have looked well, but couldn't stand up without leaning on a wall because I was so weak and dizzy. My short-term memory was fouled up. Concentrating and thinking was a chore and trying to read was difficult. I wondered if I had early onset of Alzheimer's. I was depressed and felt I was being sucked into a black hole.

I was frequently late because I had no energy to hurry and walked at a snail's pace. Still, I somehow managed to make it to work most days. I was so dedicated to the young people I worked with and was determined to continue working as long as I could sit down and work. After work, I would flop down into bed and sleep until morning. On weekends I could sometimes sleep twenty-four hours straight. At times I could not sleep at all. I alternated between long hours of sleeping and insomnia.

I scheduled appointments with specialists at the University Medical Center. Again the tests showed nothing abnormal, except for Epstein Barr Virus. I was given antibiotics which did not help, but only made me feel worse. Antibiotics feed candida. No one had checked for candida as it was rarely recognized by the medical profession at that time.

The doctor referred me to a psychiatrist who, after our first fifteen minute visit and without any testing wanted to put me on an MAO inhibitor. He suggested my symptoms were psychosomatic. I left his office quacking.

As a mental health counselor, I knew I was physically ill, not mentally ill. True, I suffered from depression, but I also knew depression is caused by chemical imbalance, by anger turned inward, feeling trapped, guilty, and loss. All natural feelings when you have a serious illness. I now know these symptoms are common with Chronic Fatigue because it attacks the central nervous system.

Another Chronic Fatigue patient said to me, "Chronic Fatigue is not death, but it takes your life away."

When I first became ill, I had my blood checked at a health food store where they were doing microscopy. They called it live cell analysis which involved taking a sample of my blood and magnifying it about 20,000 times. On the monitor I watched my blood cells and saw little parasites swimming around in my blood stream. When I approached my doctor about this he said it wasn't possible to have parasites in your blood and told me I was probably just suffering from stress and depression.

I felt useless, guilty, and life seemed hopeless. I couldn't cope with our household of teenagers. Perhaps my own children felt abandoned. They had lost their father and now their mother was not only emotionally unavailable, but physically unable to cope.

My new husband was emotionally supportive and knew I was ill, he had little energy to help me because his health also started to decline. He had kidney problems. After teaching school all day he came home exhausted and would fall asleep on the bed.

One day I ran into an old friend I hadn't seen in several years. She didn't recognize me at first. "It's Patty," I reminded her.

"Patty? What has happened to you? Your aura-your light is gone."

I had worked with her when I was an enthusiastic, energetic coordinator of a women's education resource center where I counseled and taught self-sufficiency skills. Now, I had CFIDS and was only a shell of what I once was. Prolonged stress has a way of zapping your immune system. Several hundred women went through our program and many came into the program as little ducklings, filled with fear and afraid to go into the water and face their future. I tried to instill them with hope and direction. I knew they could do it because I had been a single parent of seven children who returned to school and completed my bachelor's and master's degrees.

I had been widowed while expecting my fourth child. Three years later I married a man who was physically and verbally abusive to me and my children. We had one child together and when our son was nine months old I filed for divorce. Shortly after I found I was pregnant. I chose to stay in the marriage and ended up having twins, precious little girls.

Twins did not change his abusive behavior and when they were three months old I followed through with the divorce. I had seven children, three under 18 months old. I survived.

That was then, now I had an entirely new challenge. During the first year my CFIDS symptoms did not improve. It was impossible to find a doctor who could help me. Toward the end of the second year, there were days I started feeling better and was elated that I had energy. My health was recovering. It felt like I had returned from the living dead. It was exhilarating! Then I would overdo, and suddenly I would be as ill as ever. Scrubbing the floor, vacuuming or a walk around the block could put me into a tailspin. Another year passed and I still could not find a doctor who could help me.

I turned to chiropractors, naturopaths, and Alternative Medicine. I spent a fortune on nutritional supplements and homeopathics. Nothing helped!

For three years the chaos in our home continued and my health did not improve. My mother suffered a stroke and my siblings wanted me to help care for her in her home. My refusal alienated me from my family, but I could barely make it to work, let alone help my own children.

Summer came and I had time off work, but the stress at home was intolerable. While sitting in church one Sunday, the power went off which was quite unusual. The bright lights that illuminated the room went out, the air conditioner stopped. In the quiet I heard a still small voice say to me, "You need to leave. You need to leave." My doctor had advised me to take a vacation and get away from all of my stress but I felt that I couldn't leave my responsibilities behind. Again, I heard the voice in my head say, "You need to leave."

I started evaluating my options. My oldest daughter lived in Long Beach, California and had pleaded with me to visit her. I had another friend in San Diego, and another near San Luis Obispo that I could visit so I left home. Miraculously, the escape from five challenging teenagers, all pulling in a different directions and the pressure of trying to sell my home, turned into a spiritual journey I hadn't anticipated.

Somehow, I managed to drive to California, making short stops along the way to rest. Along the way, I listened to recordings of the scriptures and beautiful classical and inspirational music that touched my heart.

Since my daughter lived only fifteen minutes from the ocean, I spent part of each day sitting on the beach or walking slowly through the sand as warm waves nipped at my feet. The ocean energized me and recharged my spiritual batteries, batteries that had been so dim my friend had not even recognized me.

Even more energizing were the people I met. During my two weeks in California and quite by accident, I met thirty people I seemed to have a spiritual connection to. In every case, after our conversations, we each felt closer to God. There was an amazing synchronicity in our meetings and I felt an overwhelming love for each of these people. Even more amazing was the physical and spiritual healing that came into my life. I was on the road to remission.

Then a call came from home. My husband was having some chest pain and they had scheduled an angioplasty for the following morning. I left my car at the airport and flew back home that night. Fortunately, they were able to open his blocked artery. After the procedure he felt better than he felt in months.

However, for me it was a set-back, not back to the drop-dead, flu-like symptoms, but the extreme fatigue and aching started all over. When I returned to work, the stress of registering and counseling a case load of four-hundred students enhanced my CFIDS symptoms.

A friend referred me to a physician who worked with Chronic Fatigue patients. The waiting list was long, but worth the wait. He knew immediately I had CFIDS and Fibromyalgia. He understood my fatigue because his son also suffered from Chronic Fatigue and had been unable to work for six years. He wanted to put me on medical disability, but I refused. After several office visits I told him, "I either want to get better or I want to die."

It wasn't that I felt suicidal, but four years of feeling like I had been run over by a Mack semi-truck had worn me down. I had to work because we needed the money and medical insurance, but I was so fatigued and stressed it was becoming almost impossible. We discovered that my husband's kidneys were not functioning properly and he was also having more problems with his heart.

My physician wrote me a prescription for Diflucan, a medication used to treat candida, yeast and fungus problems. It was the beginning of my recovery and my passport back to the living..

Within six months my husband suffered a heart attack and had open heart surgery. I had to be well to take care of him. He had coronary artery disease and congestive heart failure. Four months later he needed another angioplasty. His physician told me his heart was so damaged he would be unable to have more surgery and that he probably wouldn't live more than two years. His doctor didn't tell him about the prognosis, nor did I . He didn't want to know. If he knew how fragile his life was, he didn't want to talk about it. He had to take an early retirement from his teaching.

During the next few years our teenagers grew up--some went off to college, a few married and we only had a few living at home which should have been less stressful, but every chest pain my husband had was like walking on egg shells for me. There was always the question *could this be a fatal heart attack?*

In the spring, I found I had liver cancer. Although it was small, both my doctor and I knew that because of my fragile immune system I could not do chemotherapy. It would kill me.

One day, while thinking I was going to die, I walked into a church. I was all alone in a hall facing a large portrait of the Savior. As I looked into his eyes, I heard him say to me, "You are going to be okay."

My doctor, along with several other alternative practitioners, put me on a vegan diet. In addition, I took cloves, black walnut extract, and wormwood to kill the many parasites that were in my blood. Everyday I juiced green vegetables and carrots, and drank four glasses a day. My skin had an orange tint. In three months the parasites in my blood were gone. Within six months my liver enzymes were normal. That was sixteen years ago. Today, I am still vegetarian, but consume no dairy.

My health improved. My husband's did not. Within the next four years he had kidney cancer and multiple heart problems. His right kidney was removed and because his other kidney was not working well, he went immediately on dialysis. After the surgery his life hung by a thread because of his heart problems. More than once he was brought back to life.

There is no quality of life on dialysis and not much when you have coronary artery disease and congestive heart failure, but put the two together and it is heart wrenching. Still, he fought courageously to live, complained little, and lived four years longer than his doctor had predicted.

Within six months of his death, I experienced Chronic Fatigue again. This time my doctor insisted I take several months of sick leave. After the sick leave, my symptoms were not as severe, but it still took me about a year to recover.

In many instances, stress had been a precursor to my fatigue so I retired from my work as a school counselor which was helpful in my recovery.

My intention was to never marry again, but an old high school friend who was also widowed and had been a neighbor to my aunt came into my life. After a whirlwind courtship with this kind, good, and gentle man, we married. Within a year my husband and I were on a mission in Florida. A year into the mission, I was again diagnosed with CFIDS and Fibromyalgia and given a prescription for Diflucan. After five days I experienced severe kidney pain and was taken off the medication.

It was then I met two sister missionaries who were drinking a green drink that resembled swamp water and claimed it gave them more energy. They introduced me to *The pH Miracle*, a book by Dr. Robert Young and to "SuperGreens," a green powder consisting of grasses, sprouted grains, and green vegetables that I mixed in distilled water and then added a few drops of an alkaline solution of sodium chlorite. Amazingly, the first day I started on the diet, drank two to three liters of the alkaline drink and had more energy. Each day I felt better. The more alkaline my diet, the more energy I had.

For twelve years I had been trying to lose the twenty pounds I gained during my first bout with CFIDS. I had tried every kind of diet with no success. The first month on the alkaline diet, I ate a whole avocado every day and lost ten pounds. Over the next few months I lost the additional ten pounds. According to Dr. Young, when the body is acidic, the acidity in our blood and tissues starts to attack our organs. In order to protect the organs, the body stores fat. "We are not overweight, we are overly acidic," claims Dr. Young.

It has been nearly five years and I now have more energy than when I was thirty and am still twenty pounds lighter.

Chapter 2

CANDIDA:
A MAJOR PLAYER IN CFIDS
AND FIBROMYALGIA

A fter my rapid recovery from CFIDS/FMS, I had a great passion to complete my doctorate in Holistic Nutrition and help others improve their physical and mental health. Having completed my courses at Clayton College, I began working on my doctoral dissertation. The title of my dissertation was *Nutritional Lifestyle Changes and Their Effect on Chronic Fatigue and Fibromyalgia.*

Researching this topic, I found physicians and researchers who believe that candida is a major player in CFIDS and FMS, as it was for me.

The booklet, *The Candida Yeast Answer,* says "Yeast is a strong invasive parasite that attaches itself to the intestinal wall and becomes a permanent resident of your internal organs. It is an integral part of life. It is present in food, and is found on exposed surfaces and in the air we breathe. Candida yeast intake and exposure cannot be avoided. Only when yeast becomes dominant in various parts of the body does it begin to present a serious health problem, resulting in disease, pain, and discomfort."

Minor increases in intestinal yeast are usually not a problem, but if yeast overgrowth is left unchallenged it can change into a mycelial fungus with rhizoids (tentacle-like projections) that penetrate the lining of the intestinal tract. These projections can cause intestinal permeability and leak toxins across the cellular membranes. This can cause a disruption in the absorption of nutrients and nutritional deficiencies that can lead to reduced immunity and weaken the body's defense systems.

Without proper nutrition, the body can't heal or regenerate its tissues and if you cannot digest and assimilate food, the tissues will eventually starve, states Dr. Robert Young, author of *The pH Miracle*.

When excessive yeast migrates to the blood stream it may cause irritability, mood swings, headaches, migraines, brain fog, inability to concentrate, poor memory, confusion, dizziness, MS-like symptoms such as slurred speech and muscle incordination, depression, and many more symptoms.

In addition to that list are:

- Fatigue or feeling drained
- Muscle aches
- Pain or swelling in joints
- Abdominal pain, gas, bloating or IBS
- Endometriosis
- Mood swings as mentioned and in some cases, Bipolar Disorder
- PMS (premenstrual syndrome)

Candida albicans is the root cause to many ailments and conditions, but is rarely diagnosed, according to Dr. Jacob Teitlebaum, author of *From Fatigued to Fantastic.* "There are no definitive tests for yeast overgrowth that will distinguish yeast overgrowth from normal yeast growth in the body. There is one test that may be useful though. This is a urine tartaric acid test. Tartaric acid is a waste product of yeast overgrowth."

Teitlebaum also feels that Dr. Crook's yeast questionnaire is a good way to determine if you have candida. The candida questionnaire can be pulled up on the internet at: http://cassia.org/candida.htm.

Dr. William Shaw, head of the Great Plains Laboratory in Kansas City, Missouri, has found elevations in urine tartaric acid in both CFIDS/FMS patients and autistic children."

Routine blood tests cannot accurately test for candida or yeast, but a special blood test called either Canishphere or candisphere can. Microscopy will also show if there is candida or yeast in the blood. Dr. Crook's book, *The Yeast Connection*, is an excellent resource and has a candida questionnaire.

Many women I know have suspected they have candida and have gone to their doctor for a blood test only to be told the results showed no candida or yeast problems, yet they still struggle with their health and chronic fatigue and fibromyalgia.

When I was meeting with Support Groups for those with CFIDS and FMS, almost without exception, all of them had candida. The symptoms of CFIDS and FMS are similar, especially fatigue and pain. In fact, 70% of patients diagnosed with FMS also meet all of the diagnostic criteria for CFS. Those with FMS tend to have more muscle pain, while CFS patients report disabling fatigue as their main symptom. (Murphree, 2003, p. 17) Not everyone that has FMS has CFIDS, but almost everyone with CFIDS has fibromyalgia.

Dr. Carol Jessop, a researcher, has reported that over 80 percent of CFIDS patients she studied will have evidence of candida determined by stain scraping taken from the mouth. Dr. Jessop presented case studies of CFIDS patients and reported findings that 80 percent of these patients had a history of recurrent antibiotic treatment.

When you take broad-spectrum antibiotics, in addition to attacking the infections they also kill friendly flora or the good bacteria in the intestines. Candida yeasts are not killed by antibiotics so they now have free reign to multiply rapidly. In the process, these yeasts release toxins that weaken the immune system. This causes repeated infections for which you take more antibiotics and a vicious cycle develops.

Fatigue is the result of cellular interference. Two things that cause fatigue are negative contaminants and the decreased presence of quality nutrients. If there were no toxic pollution factors within the blood and tissues and all necessary energy components such as blood sugar, B vitamins, sodium, potassium, magnesium, oxygen, hormones, and enzymes were available to every cell, you would have little fatigue.

In a 1982 article in *The American Journal of Medicine*, two doctors from Stanford University, Drs. William Hauser and Jack Remington, reported that some antibiotics have the ability to alter the immune response. "Tetracycline was shown to inhibit the ability of white cells to move to engulf and destroy bacteria (phagocytosis) and to delay the ability of white cells to move to the site of infection. Sulfonamides inhibited the microbiocidal activity of white cells. Trimethoprim-sulfamethoxazole inhibited antibody production. Similar action of numerous antibiotics was reported." (Schmidt, et al, 1994, p. 25)

In my case, as a teenager I had Bell's Palsy. The treatment at that time was antibiotics. For six weeks I was given daily injections of penicillin. During my adult years I had recurring doses of antibiotics that further weakened my immune system. Candida yeasts which live normally in the intestinal tract, multiply rapidly when antibiotics are taken.

But antibiotics may not be the only medication at fault. Ellen Grant, a British gynecologist states, "Candidasis is at least doubled among birth control users…"

Dr. Murray R. Susser, of Santa Monica, California, believes CFIDS develops as a combined result of nutritional deficiency and of the following three factors: (1) acquired systemic infections (often as a result of excessive use of antibiotics causing candidasis and parasite overgrowth), (2) acquired toxicity (from environment, food and drugs); and (3) poor stress-coping abilities.

According to Dr. Robert Young, "Fatigue is probably the major symptom or complaint of an overly acidic body or a body overgrown with negative microforms. Microforms— yeast, fungus, and mold—rapidly deplete your supplies of B-complex vitamins, iron, and other minerals. Microforms are the major players in chronic fatigue syndrome, which may involve yeast and fungus damage to nerve tissue and interference with nerve transmission thanks to breakdown of neurotransmitters."

Dr. Leon Chaitow, of London, England, believes that bowel toxemia, infestation of fungi, protozoa, and parasites are other factors which contribute to CFIDS and FMS. He also adds to that list, hormonal imbalances (particularly in the thyroid), and mercury toxicity from dental amalgams. (*Alternative Medicine,* 1997, p. 617)

Malabsorption problems are common in people with CFIDS and FMS. In fact, many patients with these disorders have Irritable Bowel Syndrome(IBS). The possible role of candida and yeasts in non-immune compromised individuals is disputed and was the subject of a review. However, there is increasing evidence that yeasts can cause IBS-symptoms in sensitized patients via candida. Jacob Teitlebaum, M.D., writes, "I feel most people who have irritable bowel syndrome, or 'spastic colon', have yeast overgrowth or parasites." He goes on to say, "The best marker I have found for recurrent yeast overgrowth (candida) is a return of bowel symptoms, with gas, bloating, diarrhea, or constipation."

According to Dr. Robert Young, yeast and fungus can't thrive in an alkaline environment. Microforms thrive in ...acidity. If the body is acidic, "all you need to do is balance your blood and tissue pH with nutritional supplements and an alkaline diet. When your body goes from acid back to base, yeast, fungus, and mold stop growing and revert to being benign. Their leftover toxins can then be bound up by certain fats and minerals and eliminated from the body."

Chapter 3

pH BALANCE IN THE BODY

*A*ll foods and liquids have a pH value and can be measured. Like currency which we can deposit or withdraw from a bank, foods we eat that are acidic withdraw energy from our body while foods that are alkaline deposit energy.

The pH scale ranges from 0 on the acidic end to 14 on the alkaline end. A solution is neutral if its pH is 7. The healthy pH range of oxygenated arterial blood is 7.35 to 7.45, and that of the carbon dioxide-laden venous blood is 7.35 to 7.41. To remain viable the body must remain slightly alkaline. Even minor variations from these values are biologically costly.

According to Dr. Robert Young, the most important single measurement to your health is the pH of your blood and tissues: how acidic or alkaline is it? The body will go to great lengths to balance and preserve a mildly basic or alkaline level in our blood and tissues. Chronic over acidity corrodes body tissue, and if unchecked will interrupt all cellular functions from the beating of your heart to the neural firing of your brain.

Overacidity attacks every organ in the body, even the thyroid. According to Teitlebaum, the thyroid gland is the body's gas pedal. It slows or speeds the metabolism. An under active thyroid (producing too little hormone), common in CFIDS/FMS, is signified by symptoms of fatigue, achiness, weight gain, poor mental functioning, and intolerance to cold. (Teitlebaum, 2001, p. 14)

Dr. Robert Young believes that over-acidification of body fluids and tissues underlie almost all disease. If tissue pH deviates too far to the acid side, oxygen levels decrease and cellular metabolism will stop.

"An aberrant virus, fungus or bacteria in the body can only survive in an acid environment. When acid-forming levels of the body are under control, candida albicans will normalize itself. A malevolent opportunistic virus, bacteria, or fungus feeds only on a body that provides food for it—body laden with tissue acid waste products." (Baroody, 2002, pp. 141-142)

According to researchers Jaffe and Brown, our immune defense and repair mechanisms and a host of cell and system enzyme catalysts, all do their best in an exquisitely narrow pH range.

Jay A. Goldstein MD, has discovered that the activation of some neural receptors in the brain (NMDA N-methyl-D-aspartate) can be inhibited by pH. "As the environment around the receptor channel becomes more acidic, receptor activity is suppressed, so at a pH of 6.0, receptor activation is suppressed nearly completely." (Goldstein, 2004, p. 229)

"Alkalinization enhances the function of some neurotransmitters, especially N-type $Ca2+$ channels, the most important for regulating neurotransmitter release. Neurotransmitters are substances that transmit nerve impulses to the brain." (Goldstein, 2004, p. 155) With decreasing pH, cerebral metabolic rate (brain activity) decreases.

The concept of brain abnormalities contributing to CFIDS/FMS is something which has long been suspected. (Bell, 1995, p. 116)

A common characteristic of people with FMS is that they report a high amount of pain. Dr. Goldstein believes, "Acidosis, local or systemic, increases pain by activating channels in sensory neurons." The more acidic the body, the more pain experienced.

Also, FMS patients with indications of acidosis or lactic acid are much more likely to have a lactate induced panic attack. (Goldstein, 2004, p.93)

Chronic acidity attacks our organs, tissues, brain and all systems in the body. This is why pH is so vitally important.

How do we measure pH?

The pH of your saliva or urine can be measured at home with pH strips which are available at most health food stores or pharmacies. Since the saliva is much more variable, it is best to test your urine pH first thing in the morning as both your saliva and urine can change according to what you eat.

What affects our body pH?

The foods we eat and our stressful life style are the main factors that create acid in our body. Our body fluids should be in a range close to 7.36 (slightly alkaline); an acidic environment is anything less than that.

Fatigue is the result of cellular interference. Two things that cause fatigue are negative contaminants and the decreased presence of quality nutrients. If there were no toxic pollution factors within the blood and tissues and all necessary energy components such as blood sugar, B vitamins, sodium, potassium, magnesium, oxygen, hormones, and enzymes were available to every cell, you would have little fatigue.

In a clinical study by the Osteoporosis Education Project, directed by Susan Brown and Dr. Russell Jaffe, it was implicated that the contemporary Western Diet leads to chronic, low-level acidosis.

The major recognized sources of net acid load in the body are:

1. Diet

    a. Protein consumption above 60 grams a day

    b. Dietary phosphate/phosphoric acid (soft drinks)

    c. Dietary sulfate

    d. Long-chain fatty acids in excess of 15%-20% of total dietary calories.

2. Distress (raises excess cortisol and adrenaline).

The Brown and Jaffe study also found that these factors can result not only in detriment of basic health and well-being, but also in significant bone and body mineral loss. Acidosis forces the loss of alkalizing sodium, potassium, carbonate, calcium, magnesium, and other minerals from bone stores and from the body.

Bone is sensitive to small changes in pH. In vitro studies document that even one-tenth of a point drop in pH does the following.

1. Greatly stimulates osteoclastic (bone reabsorption) activity.

2. Inhibits osteoblastic (bone-building) action; and

3. Induces a multifold bone and body mineral loss."

Solution:

In a study of vegetarian and animal protein diets, it was found that urinary pH was more acidic in those consuming animal protein. Brown & Jaffe believe the solution to this problem lies in a return to a diet rich in alkaline foods.

The basis of an alkaline diet is green rich leafy green vegetables. They are overflowing with phytonutrients, fiber, enzymes, and antioxidants such as vitamin E. Not only do they lower the risk of cognitive decline, these vegetables also help give you more energy, support your immune system, promote healthy digestion, and improve overall health.

How can you center your meals around leafy green vegetables? Eat salads with dark green lettuce; sauté spinach with garlic for a gourmet side-dish. Serve lightly steamed collards, kale, and mustard greens and serve with tofu cubes that have been baked with onions, garlic and ¼ cup of Bragg Liquid Aminos. The possibilities are endless.

Alkalizing foods include avocado, beets, bell peppers, broccoli, cabbage, romaine, jicama, carrots, cauliflower, dark lettuce, garlic, kale, leeks, onion, parsley, squash, tomato, zucchini, lemon, lime, grapefruits, and cucumber (one of the most alkalizing foods you can eat).

Jay A. Goldstein, MD, author of *Tuning the Brain*, has seen over 20,000 patients at the Chronic Fatigue Institutes in California. For those who need a jump start, Dr. Goldstein states, "I alkalinize some patients with citrate (Polycitra-K). Citrates, in the form of sodium citrate or potassium citrate, are alkalinizing agents, but potassium citrate in the form of Polycitra-K does not impose a sodium load on the body. Additional sodium can contribute to high blood pressure. The treatment option of

Polycitra-K is simple and not particularly expensive or hazardous. (Goldstein, 2004, p. 229)

Chapter 4

THE CHINA STUDY

The Dangers of Meat and Dairy

*T*he China Study," by Dr. T. Colin Campbell, one of the world's most respected nutrition authorities, is the largest and most comprehensive study ever done on diet, disease and nutrition. *The New York Times* called it the "Grand Prix," of nutrition. After 34 years of solid scientific research, his findings indicate that advanced heart disease, relatively advanced cancers of certain types, diabetes and a few other degenerative diseases can be reversed by diet. *The China Study* was the culmination of a twenty year partnership with Cornell University, Oxford University and the Chinese Academy of Preventive Medicine and was funded by the National Institutes of Health.

Campbell's interest was peaked about the effect of diet on disease when he was doing a nationwide project in the Philippines working with malnourished children. Their goal was to have the children consume more corn and peanuts to increase the consumption of protein. At the time, the Philippines had a high prevalence of liver cancer among children and it was assumed this was among the poor children. At first, the team working with Campbell thought the cause of liver cancer could be a mold toxin called aflatoxin found in peanuts and corn (also in stored wheat and grains), something they had not been aware of prior to the study. Aflatoxin has been called one of the most potent carcinogens ever discovered. The project to feed more corn and peanuts was soon abolished and more research was done. Surprisingly, Collin found the children who ate the highest-protein diets were the ones most likely to get liver cancer. They were from the wealthiest families.

Dr. Campbell then found research from India that had studied two groups of rats. To one group, they administered high doses of aflatoxin and fed them a diet of 20% animal protein, a level that many of us consume in the West. In the other group they gave the same carcinogenic amount of aflatoxin, but fed this group of rats a diet of only 5% protein. Every animal that consumed the 20% protein diet had evidence of liver cancer, and every single animal that consumed only 5% animal protein (sometimes casein from milk), avoided liver cancer. Dr. Campbell and his group replicated this study over and over, always with the same results.

The team then studied the diets of over 6500 people from 64 counties in China. This was a longitudinal study lasting over 30 years. Blood and urine tests were repeatedly taken from all participants. Researchers spent time in the homes to determine the diets and foods participants were eating. Environmental issues were examined. There were over 8000 statistically significant results from this study.

The evidence to support that animal protein increased tumor development while nutrients from plant-based foods decreased tumor development was statistically significant throughout all of the studies.

Campbell writes, "We now have a deep and broad range of evidence showing that a whole foods, plant-based diet is best for cancer." But, he doesn't stop there; he includes other diseases such as heart disease, diabetes, autoimmune diseases, kidneys, bones, eyes and brains.

Meat is one of the most acidic foods that we eat and acidity can create havoc with our immune system and overall health.

America's health is failing even though we spend more per capita on health care than any other society in the world. Two-thirds of Americans are overweight and one-third or our children are either overweight or at risk of becoming so. More than 15 million Americans have diabetes and will fall prey to heart disease as often as we did thirty years ago. The War on

Cancer is a continuous battle. "The issues all come down to three things, breakfast, lunch and dinner."

Chapter 5

DIET TO HELP ELIMINATE YEAST

A first step in treating yeast conditions is to avoid sugar and other sweets--soft drinks, corn syrup, pastries, candy, jellies, honey, fructose, most fruits, white flours, products with yeast in them, and most ready-to-eat cereals. Do not use mushrooms (fruiting bodies of yeast and fungus), vinegar, alcoholic beverages, fermented foods, or dairy products. Instead of dairy products you can drink, almond milk, rice milk, or organic soy milk. It is important to use organic soy otherwise it may be genetically engineered.

Raw almonds, Brazil nuts, flax seeds, filberts, Macadamia nuts, pecans, pine nuts, Pumpkin seeds, sesame and sunflower seeds are good sources for protein and Vitamin E. They also contain the greatest source of essential fatty acids. If possible, buy organic nuts and seeds from special suppliers. The best way to eat seeds or nuts is to soak them overnight to start the sprouting process, which makes the fats and proteins more digestible and enhances enzymes. Nuts and seeds should be stored in the refrigerator to prevent oils from going rancid.

Lemons, limes, grapefruit, tomatoes and avocadoes are good fruits you are encouraged to use. Suggested grains include quinoa (high in protein), millet, buckwheat, kamut, spelt, basmati brown rice, wild rice, and soba noodles. Also, use unprocessed organic or natural foods, freshly juiced vegetables, young coconut milk, and distilled or purified water.

According to Dr. Joseph Issels, protein, fat, carbohydrates and other nutrients are transformed by the digestive process into low-molecular water soluble compounds. These react either acidically or basically and can alter chemical reactions of body fluids. Since the body can only function normally when the reaction of fluids is balanced, a constant supply of only acidic or basic food would be harmful. An "acid-base equilibrium" is maintained by a correct choice of foods. Base-formers are all kinds of vegetables and some fruits, while acid-formers are all cereals, flours, puddings, bread, cakes, dairy products, cheese, and all kinds of meat and fish. The acid-base balance can be ensured if each meal consists of eighty percent base- formers and twenty percent acid-formers. (Issels, 1999, p. 149)

According to the Brown & Jaffe Study, guidelines for an alkaline diet are as follows:

1. The bulk of the diet should be alkalizing vegetables, fruits, lentils, nuts, seeds and spices. Sixty to 80% of foods eaten should be alkaline.

2. Limit animal flesh to four ounces per day, and restrict total protein intake to 60 grams or less per day. Sixty grams is about the size of two fish fillets. Beef is heavier, so would be a smaller portion.

3. Maintain a fat intake of no more than 15% to 20% of total calorie intake.

4. Drink 64 ounces of high mineral (highly dissolved solids) spring water daily.

5. Fresh vegetable juice is an exceptionally good source of buffering minerals. Those with low-grade acidosis might drink 2-3 eight ounce glasses a day. Sixteen to 24 ounces of juice from organic vegetables would be sufficient to correct for 40 to 50mEg of excess organic acid.

Use alkalizing nutritional supplements.

6. Alkalizing supplements include bioavailable, ionized minerals and a high quality, antigen-free acorbate buffered with calcium, magnesium, zinc, and potassium. Add L-glutamine with pyriodoxal alphaketoglutarate (PAK) Kreb's salts, cesium, rubidium, and sesame/flax seeds as needed to keep a healthy first-morning urine pH.

7. Modify the diet and supplement sufficiently to obtain and maintain a first-morning pH of 6.5 to 7.5, which may reflect the existence of adequate buffering mineral reserves.

8. Reverse learned patterns of distress by practicing relaxation responses, enjoyable activities, and weight-bearing activities.

It is well-known there is some decline in brain power as we age, but scientists have now found that there's a surprising way to significantly slow that decline: eating more vegetables-but not just any vegetables. The real "brain boosting" nutrients are found in the leafy greens such as spinach, kelp, collard greens, and kale.

In a recent study published in the journal, Neurology, researchers from Rush University in Chicago discovered that eating an average of 2.8 or more servings of vegetables a day over a six-year period slowed cognitive decline by 38 to 40 percent. While all kinds of vegetables were included in this study, those that provided the most powerful protection were leafy greens.

Many people I have counseled are not ready to change their diet. Some have said, "I would rather die than change my diet."

After my friend had a heart attack, he sought my advice, I asked what he had been eating. His diet included lots of meat, saturated fat, chips, fried foods, cream cheese and bagels, and ice cream. My comment was, "That's what you are feeding your face. What are you feeding your body?"

Some people are on the edge of life and death because of their food choices. In effect, they are on the train track and the train is coming. It is their choice to stand there (eat themselves into oblivion), or get off the tracks (make some healthy life style changes).

Pain can be caused by inflammation. Sugar causes inflammation, and that includes all sugars including honey, fructose, and syrups.

It has been said, "live food–live body, dead food–dead body." Eating raw foods sustains the body in much the same way the sun sustains the earth. We do not get energy or enzymes from dead food. Processed and refined foods are dead foods and nutritionally deficient.

A raw food diet improves digestion. Raw food digests marvelously well and does not produce the acid, bile and residual effects of digestion that go with a cooked food diet. A raw food diet is based on unprocessed and uncooked plant foods, such as fresh fruit and vegetables, sprouts, seeds, nuts, grains, beans, nuts, and seaweed.

Why switch from cooked foods to more raw foods? The answer is simple: for optimal health this kind of diet is full of foods that nourish or fuel the body with life-giving force (i.e. enzymes, electric or vital energy, chlorophyll, minerals, vitamins, etc.), thereby strengthening, energizing and building it, without depleting or causing any hindrance to its functions.

Heating food above 116 degrees F is believed to destroy enzymes which assist in the digestion and absorption of food. Enzymes as well as vitamins, minerals, and proteins are completely destroyed at approximately 130 degrees F. Cooking also diminishes the nutritional value and "life force" of food. At least 3/4 of food consumed should not be heated over 116 degrees F.

Dangers of Microwave Ovens

I don't cook any food in a microwave oven. In Dr. Lita Lee's book, *Health Effects of Microwave Radiation - Microwave Ovens*, she states that every microwave oven leaks electro-magnetic radiation, harms food and converts substances cooked in it to dangerous organ-toxic and carcinogenic products. Microwave ovens are far more harmful than previously imagined. Here are a few findings of the German and Russian investigators:

Decrease in Food Value – Microwave exposure caused significant decreases in the nutritive value of all foods researched. There was a decrease in bioavailability of B-complex vitamins, vitamin C, vitamin E, essential minerals and lipotropics in all foods, a loss of 60 to 90% of the vital energy field of all tested foods, and a marked acceleration of structural disintegration in all foods.

Biological Effects of Exposure — Microwave exposure causes a breakdown of the human "life-energy field." Other effects include degeneration and circuit breakdowns within the front portion of the brain where thought and higher functions reside, loss of balance, long term cumulative loss of vital energy and long-lasting residual effects.

Nine reasons to throw out your microwave oven (taken from research):

1. Continually eating food processed from a microwave oven causes long term, permanent, brain damage by "shorting out" electrical impulses in the brain (de-polarizing or de-magnetizing the brain tissue).

2. The human body cannot metabolize (breakdown) the unknown by-products created in microwaved food.

3. The effects of microwaved food by-products are residual (long term, permanent) within the human body.

4. Minerals, vitamins, and nutrients of all microwaved food are reduced or altered so that the human body gets little or no benefit, or the human body absorbs altered compounds that cannot be broken down.

5. The minerals in vegetables are altered into cancer-causing free radicals when cooked in microwave ovens.

6. Microwaved foods cause stomach and intestinal cancerous growths (tumors). This may explain the rapid increased rate of colon cancer in America.

7. Prolonged eating of microwaved foods causes cancerous cells to increase.

8. Continual ingestion of microwaved food causes immune system deficiencies through lymph gland and serum alterations.

9. Eating microwaved food causes loss of memory, concentration, emotional instability, and a decrease of intelligence.

Standing in front of a microwave is also highly damaging to your health. Perhaps you have already felt this intuitively. Although a door and rubber seals try to contain the microwaves in the oven, they aren't 100% successful.

I cannot over estimate how important it is to eat more raw foods. The main difference between raw foods and cooked foods is enzymes! Enzymes aid the body in the digestive process because they break down the food in order for it to be absorbed into our blood-stream. There are billions of cells in the human body, each doing a particular task. After they complete their task, these cells are left completely depleted and need to be replenished. Raw foods are full of living enzymes that replace the exhausted cells

Start changing your diet slowly. Begin by adding green drinks and alkalizing agents. Some people experience a detoxification reaction when they start a raw food diet, especially if their previous diet included a lot of meat, sugar, and caffeine. Mild headaches, nausea, and cravings can occur but usually only last for several days.

Also, drink lots of water. Dr. Young says, "When we are born, we are 90% water. When we die, we are 50% water. We literally die of dehydration."

Heavy Metals and Candida

I recently talked to a doctor who said that heavy metals in the body will contribute to candida. A green liquid diet or pureed diet for several days will help eliminate heavy metals from the body. Also, a foot bath detox will pull toxins and heavy metals from the body.

Chapter 6

POSITIVE RESULTS OF AN ALKALINE
DIET ON CFIDS/FMS PATIENTS

$\mathcal{F}$ or my doctoral dissertation, I originally started with twenty four people who had either been diagnosed with CFIDS and FMS, CFIDS, or FMS, who agreed to participate in the study. However, only eight participated in the project. Originally all of these individuals were unable to work or had limited activity because of their illness. Each of these people had used an alkaline or whole foods, plant-based diet for at least three months. In addition, they took alkaline supplements which consisted mainly of a green drink containing barley, lemon, wheat, and other greens, and Prime pH drops (sodium chlorite), which is an alkalizing agent. This drink provided over 125 vitamins and minerals, along with amino acids. Subjects drank from one to four liters of this drink daily in order to alkalize and flush toxins from the body.

On a Likert scale, each of the eight participants measured sixteen symptoms after being on the alkaline diet. Seven out of eight individuals had excellent improvement in energy, with one experiencing moderate improvement. All subjects had outstanding improvement in the elimination and reduction of symptoms. All experienced excellent to good improvement in decreased joint and muscle pain. One hundred percent of the participants for whom these symptoms were problematic experienced improvement in 13 out of 16 symptoms. All of the people were able to return to their normal activities.

Other Success Stories

This is the story of my 80-year-old father, who at his advanced age has changed his diet to be alkaline.

> On February 8, 2007 my father had a heart attack and subsequent heart surgery requiring a whopping six bypasses. He was very ill and nearly died twice in the days after the surgery. He has been a diabetic for nearly 30 years. Diabetics must monitor their blood sugars carefully and there is a quarterly blood test called the glycosylated hemoglobin A1C test (HbA1c). This reading reveals your average blood glucose level over the past three months and can be used

to predict your risk for diabetes complications-including heart attack. The goal number on this test is 7.1 or lower. In his own words my father explains what has happened since changing his diet:

My HbA1c readings before cardiac surgery were between 7.1 and 8 for years. Thirty days after surgery and after being on an alkaline diet without animal fats or proteins, my HbA1c dropped to 6.1. I also lost 10 pounds during the same period.

My general practitioner, Dr. Clark, while giving me my quarterly diabetes checkup, noted these changes and told me my chance of having a heart attack had dropped by a factor of ten. He showed me a chart in his office of the probability of heart attack vs. blood sugar levels. There was a sharp drop in heart attack risk in the area between 5.9 and 6.9 on the HbA1c test. His figure of 10% was an estimate taken from the chart. It means that of a group of 100 men of my age with their HbA1c at 6.1, if 50 of them would have a heart attack in the next 12 months, by reducing their HbA1c to 6.1, only 5 would be likely to have heart attack in that time.

Still following the general guidelines [of an alkaline diet] we set up, my weight continues to drop. I weighed 213 pounds as I entered the hospital four months ago. Yesterday I was 182.

At my four month post-heart attack exam my cardiologist, said my condition was excellent. Regarding the weight loss and how it has been attained, he said, "It is the right way to go, but it is a hard way to follow."

People ask me all the time how the weight was lost. But they generally lose interest when I start to tell them. So now I say that the way to lose weight is to:

- Get to be 80
- Have a heart attack and get a by-pass
- Nearly die
- Decide it's time to make a few changes in your lifestyle

If a 17-year-old teenager and her 80-year-old grandfather can make dietary changes that give them back their health, it's not farfetched to believe that anybody can if they are willing. Though not easy at first, a return to health is worth it!

Tiffany Whitehead

Michelle was a 26-year-old who had been almost bedridden for the better part of a year. She was so weak with CFIDS/FMS that she was unable to drive. Her mother-in-law drove her to my office. Her score on the Candida Questionnaire was 243. Michelle was committed to changing her diet and started on a cleanse and an alkaline diet immediately. She also took supplements for candida. Six weeks later she called me from San Diego where she and her husband were on vacation. A few months later she went back to work.

This is an email I recently received:

Dear Patty,

I attended your class in October, bought your book and the next day I went on the alkaline diet. I mixed up salad greens in apple juice and drank those. All the fibromyalgia pain left. I am on my 7th week of eating vegan. I feel so much better. I am grateful for your class. I wanted to let you know how well I was doing. Every time I start hurting I drink a green drink made out of salad greens and water. — Pattsy Dayley

The majority of people I talk to with candida, CFIDS/FMS are not willing to change their diet. They want some magic pill or a quick fix. I had a choice to endure the pain, exhaustion, memory problems, depression and other nagging symptoms or change my diet. Today I have more energy than when I was in my twenties. Each morning I do 30 minutes of aerobic exercise on a mini-trampoline and I am free of pain.

Chapter 7

SUPPLEMENTS FOR TREATING
YEAST OVERGROWTH

*T*he following are some supplements which have been helpful in eliminating yeast overgrowth. When adding supplements to your diet, begin with only one or two supplements. Consult your pharmacist if you are taking medications to check for possible interactions between the drugs and supplement. I am very cautious about mixing drugs and herbs. Homeopathics generally have no interactions.

Grapefruit Seed Extract tablets: Helps rid the body of harmful microorganisms, viruses, yeast , and bacteria.

Olive leaf extract: A powerful healer of microbial infections, bacteria, yeast, and viruses.

Caprilyic acid: Another natural aid to eliminate candida. Recommended dosage is on the label.

Acidophilus: Use a nondairy formula and take on an empty stomach. Helps fight candida infection.

Biotin: Helps relieve muscle pain and is a good supplement to fight candida, 50 mg three times a day.

Coenzyme Q10: Improves tissue oxygenation, aids immune response, increases energy.

Para-Shield: A supplement by DaVinci Laboratory which fights candida, yeast, fungus, bacteria, parasites, and viruses. The supplement contains black walnut, wormwood, Olive leaf extract, grapefruit seed extract, Pau D Arco, black cumin and garlic. It can be ordered by calling: 1-800-325-1776

DMG-Dimethylglcine: Increases energy, boosts mental acuity, and enhances the immune system.

Fibro-DMG: A supplement for Fibromyalgia and muscle pain from DaVinci Laboratory. It contains magnesium and DMG (dimethylglcine).

Aloe vera juice: Boosts the white cells ability to kill yeast cells.

Milk Thistle: Loaded with phytochemicals and is a safe supplement with other medications. Protects the liver from other toxins and pollutants by preventing free-radical damage and stimulates the production of new liver cells. Also protects the kidneys. Good for gallbladder and adrenal disorders, inflammatory bowel problems, psoriasis, weakened immune system, and all liver disorders. Usually safe to take with medications, just not together.

Vitamin D3: An immune system modulator to support healthy T cell and macrophage responses. Vitamin D3 can be synthesized by humans in skin upon exposure to ultraviolet -B radiation from sunlight or it can be obtained from the diet. Vitamin D or sunlight is a wonderful buffer of metabolic acids which is the primary cause of some auto immune diseases. Twenty to 30 minutes a day of natural sunlight helps reduce metabolic acids.

SuperGreens or other green powder drinks. SuperGreens is what I drank during my recovery from CFIDS/FMS. It comes in powder or pill form. I added lemon juice to my mixture. I order them from Innerlight INC. at 1-800-655-0601. Barley powder is also a good source of alkalizing green drink. Avoid drinks with spirulina and chlorella. If you can tolerate wheat grass that is an excellent alkalizing agent. I have found that many people who are overly acidic cannot tolerate straight wheat grass juice.

Magnesium deficiency may also contribute to CFIDS and FMS. According to a recent study, when twenty people with CFIDS were compared with twenty healthy volunteers, the CFIDS patients' magnesium content was shown to be lower. In another study, thirty-two patients with CFIDS were given intramuscular injections of magnesium. Eighty percent of those receiving the magnesium injections had reduced symptoms and improved energy while less than 20 percent of those on placebo injections reported improvement. (Cox, et al, 1991 pp.757-760)

An article in the journal of Medical Hypothesis proposed that glutathione, an antioxidant essential for lymphocyte function, may be depleted in Chronic Fatigue patients. Glutathione is needed for both the immune system and for aerobic muscular contraction. The authors proposed that glutathione depletion by an activated immune system also causes the muscular fatigue and myalgia associated with Chronic Fatigue.

As an essential aid to health, glutathione works as the master antioxidant in our body, optimizes the white blood cells and detoxifies a long list of pollutants and carcinogens or acids. The best way to raise glutathione levels is by eating foods that are high in glutathione such as avocados.

Supplements will make very little difference if you are eating sugar in any form.

Anti-Inflammatories

Nutritional Supplements that have antiflammatory properties include: Tumeric, Yucca (a natural cortisone), MSM, Magnesium, Omega 3's , Bromelain, Pycnogenol, grape seed extract, Boswellia, fish oil, flax seed, and Ginger. Boswellia and Ginger are especially helpful for fibromyalgia pain. Remember that supplements by themselves will never be as effective as dietary change and supplements.

Homeopathics can be helpful for pain. Rhus toxicodendron helps arthritis and fibromyalgia pain. Arnica montana is good for any kind of pain, especially muscular pain and has almost no side effects. Follow the directions on the bottle and let tablets dissolve under your tongue—do not chew them. Take homeopathics ten minutes away from food. You can take tablets every fifteen minutes for the first two hours, and then four times a day. It will usually work within the first week.

Fish Oil Essential for Depression and Mental Health

Omega-3fatty acids are a safe, simple, natural treatment for depression, mental health, and enhancing mood without side effects. Andrew Stoll, a psychiatrist and director of the Psychopharmacology Research Laboratory at McClean Hospital, is author of the book *The Omega-3 Connection*. The book is designed to educate about the benefits of fish oil and help readers restore their natural balance of omega-3 fatty acids, which are found in high concentrations in the brain.

Over the past century, people in the United States have largely eliminated omega-3 fatty acids from their diet, due to the huge consumption of fried and processed foods and a low-fat diet craze.

Some fats are absolutely required for good health, while others are detrimental. The most dangerous fats are those found in margarines, shortenings, heated oils, cheese, and some meats. There is reason to be concerned about bad fats.

Sixty-eight percent of people die from three degenerative diseases that involve fatty degeneration. They include cardio-vascular disease, cancer and diabetes. We need the healing fatty acids. Omega-3s are essential for optimal function of every cell in our bodies and we cannot manufacture them internally. They can be obtained only through our diet.

Andrew Stoll, on the faculty of Harvard Medical School, was interested in alternative treatments for bipolar patients. He conducted an extensive search on medical research papers to find substances with properties similar to standard mood stabilizers, Lithium and Valproate. After he and his colleague, Dr. Emauel Severus, reviewed hundreds of papers, they pulled up one match time and again-common fish oil.

Fish oils are already known for their role in preventing heart disease, rheumatoid arthritis, and Crohn's disease. They may also be responsible for protecting against arthritis, diabetes, and some psychiatric disorders. The brain requires more omega-3 and fatty acids than any other system in the body. According to Dr. Stoll, without omega-3s, the brain cannot function normally, so even the most powerful antide-pressants will be unable to improve mood. For optimum health, omega-3 and omega-6 fatty acids should be eaten in nearly equal proportions. Omega-6 fatty acids are contained in vegetable and seed oils, including olive oil, sunflower oil, and safflower oils. Omega-3s are more difficult to obtain, and are most often from fish oil. Flax oil and seed contains some Omega-3s.

In addition, omega-3s are safe and effective supplements for pregnancy, nursing mothers, and postpartum depression. Blood levels of omega-3s decrease during the later stages of pregnancy and stay low, because the fetus receives these essential lipids preferentially (especially if there is a shortage). Lack of omega-3s can damage a mother's health after birth and cause major postpartum depression. These fatty acids are important in cell-signaling pathways, and are vital to the function of many brain systems, including the neural systems regulating mood and emotions. Research indicates that a lack of omega-3s during pregnancy may impair development of the visual system of a fetus, and may also compromise future intelligence.

There is some evidence that attention deficit-hyperactivity disorder (ADHD) might be rooted in a deficiency of the omega-3 fatty acids. Researchers noticed that in two groups of children it was found that those who had omega-3 deficiency and ADHD had similarities. Both had excess thirst, greater frequency of dry hair and skin, and an increased need to urinate. When they tested the blood levels of the ADHD subjects they found that 40 percent had low levels of omega-3s.

Omega 3 fatty acids have also been found to have anti-inflammatory and can therefore help to relieve or alleviate pain.

Dr. Stoll recommends 1 to 2 grams (1000-to 2000 milligrams) of fish oil daily for health, mood, and cognitive improvement.

Chapter 8

IRRITABLE BOWEL SYNDROME

"*I*rritable Bowel Syndrome or IBS is a digestive disorder that causes abdominal pain and can affect people of all ages, including teens and children. It is estimated that one in five adult Americans has symptoms of the disease, but fewer than half of them seek a doctor's help or diagnosis. Twice as many women as men suffer from the condition, although more men may suffer from the disease than reported because men are less likely to consult a physician. IBS is the most common digestive disorder seen by doctors.

Irritable Bowel Syndrome is a condition in which the large intestine, or colon, fails to function normally. Normal rhythmic contractions of the digestive tract become irregular which interferes with natural movement of food and waste materials. Mucus and toxins accumulate and this can create a partial obstruction of the digestive tract, trapping gas and stools. This can cause bloating, distention, and constipation, sometimes followed by diarrhea. IBS is considered a functional disorder of the colon, since there is no evidence of structural damage to the intestine.

Symptoms of IBS include pain, constipation and/or diarrhea, anorexia, gas, anxiety, nausea, depression, flatulence, intolerances to certain foods, and mucus in the stools. Because of lack of absorption of nutrients, malnutrition may result. Increased minerals and trace elements can quickly be depleted by diarrhea.

According to Brenda Watson, N.D., and Leonard Smith, M.D., authors of the *Gut Solution*, the cause of IBS is uncertain, although bacterial, fungal, or parasites may be involved. Possible causes may include, irregularities in intestinal hormones and nerves responsible for bowel motility, stress, dietary inadequacies, food intolerances, inadequate enzymes, not enough hydrochloric acid, lactose intolerance, medications, especially antibiotics which destroy the intestinal flora, and dysbiosis (too many bad bacteria, not enough good ones).

Evidence suggests food sensitivities and allergies play a major role in IBS.

Most common allergies are dairy products, wheat, corn, coffee, tea, chocolate and citrus fruits or juices. Over-consumption of alcohol and nicotine can trigger intestinal spasms.

In a study done by Dr. Chi Young, University of Iowa, it was discovered that symptoms of irritable bowel (IBS) could be triggered with increased ingestion of fructose and eliminated by avoiding it. The most common form of fructose in the American diet is corn syrup. However, other forms of sugar such as mannitol and sorbitol may cause problems for people with IBS as well.

Although the theory is controversial, Jacob Teitlebaum, M.D., author of *From Fatigued To Fantastic*, writes, "I feel most people who have irritable bowel syndrome, or 'spastic colon', have yeast overgrowth or parasites." He goes on to say, "The best marker I have found for recurrent yeast overgrowth (candida) is a return of bowel symptoms, with gas, bloating, diarrhea, or constipation." He recommends the book, *The Yeast Connection*, by Dr. William G. Crook., for more information on the subject.

The traditional treatment for IBS is dietary restrictions, stress management, and medications. Most doctors will advise the patient to gradually increase their intake of dietary fiber, including fruits, vegetables, millet, brown rice and buckwheat. James Balch, M.D., author of *Prescription for Nutritional Healing*, recommends acidophilus, flaxseed and borage oil, aloe vera juice, and proteolytic enzymes.

Balch says, avoid all butter, animal fats, coffee, caffeine and carbonated beverages, candy, chocolate, dairy products, fried foods, ice cream, wheat bran and wheat foods, sugar, nuts, and all junk and processed foods. Avoid meat because it takes longer to digest and process than fresh foods, raw foods, or lightly steamed foods. Chew your foods well, digestion begins in the mouth. Do not eat right before going to bed—wait several hours after eating before lying down.

A good supplement to help heal the bowel is called Herbal Aloe Force, which is a combination of Aloe, Essiac herbs, Cat's claw, Pau d'arco, burdock, and chamomile.

Order from Herbal Answers in Saratoga Springs, New York at 1-518-581-1968 or check the web site at: www.herbalanswers.com.

If dietary modifications yield no relief, it is wise to consult a physician because IBS symptoms are similar to those of other disorders.

Chapter 9

PAIN MANAGEMENT

*T*hirty years ago I had such severe arthritic pain I could hardly walk. My chiropractor repeatedly told me to give up sugar. At that time I thought that was nonsense. I loved almond fudge ice cream, brownies, cookies, and other goodies. But, my pain was so bad that I couldn't dance, an activity I loved. In fact I could barely get out of bed. I had a tough time sleeping, walking up and down stairs, or cleaning. I hated to move because my body ached so much. My doctor finally said to me, "Would you rather have the pain or give up the goodies?"

Pain can cause inflammation and sugar causes inflammation. That includes all sugars including honey, frutose, and syrups. Other acidic foods include vinegar and bad fats, such as any fried food, saturated or trans fatty acids, butter, and margarine. On the other hand, good fats such as Omega 3-s , which includes fish oil and flax seeds have antinflamatory properties.

I gave up the goodies—not easily, but I did it. I started doing gentle stretches then areobic exercises in a swimming pool, then swimming, and then walking. In a few months my arthritic pain was gone, never to return unless I ate sugar or white flour.

Every red blood cell in our bodies is composed of the foods we eat. The more acidic—the more lactic acid in our body, the more pain we will experience. I have found that for both me and my clients, eating alkaline foods (lots of greens) and changing our negative or stinking-thinking patterns will help our body become more alkaline.

Pain is more than just hurting. Pain decreases your physical, emotional, social, and spiritual well being in a variety of ways. It affects you physically, mentally, and emotionally. With pain, you may:

- Be less able to function
- Feel tired and lethargic
- Lose your appetite or have nausea
- Not be able to sleep, or have your sleep interrupted by pain
- Experience less enjoyment and more anxiety

- Become depressed, anxious, or unable to concentrate on anything except pain
- Feel a loss of control
- Have less interaction with friends
- Be less able to enjoy sex or affection
- Feel that you are a burden on your family

Dr. James Dillard, author of *Chronic Pain Solution* believes you don't have to live with your pain continuously. Even if you have suffered for years, you may have more options than you think. Whatever your source of pain, you can find a combination of high-tech medicine and gentle alternative therapies that help control your pain and gives you back your life.

Dr. Peter Lehndorff, owner of his own pain clinic in Fitchburg, Massachusetts, has seen many patients with severe chronic pain and developed his own theories about pain management and has looked at vitamin therapy, special exercises, nerve blocks, ointments, electric stimulators, medications, hypnosis, and counseling. Some worked for some patients while others did not.

He discovered that the patients who improved the most were those who had the urgent desire and will to improve. Attitude was the major motivating factor to get better. The mind has immense powers. Optimism is a definite positive factor. Lehndorff found four factors for positive results in pain management:

1. The patients who succeeded wanted to get better.

2. They expected to get better.

3. They worked on getting better.

4. They learned quick methods of motivation.

If you have back pain, some experts agree that the number one cause of minor back pain is poor posture. So, when you're standing, you want to keep your head up, stomach pulled in, and neck, shoulders, and pelvis in a straight line. Sitting actually puts more pressure on your back than any other position, even standing. And when we're sitting—whether it's while eating dinner, watching TV, working at the computer, or driving in the car—we often do it with our heads tilting slightly forward.

Your head rests on your neck like a golf ball on a tee. And given the average adult head weighs 8 to 10 pounds, that golf ball is more like a bowling ball. Your back and neck muscles are constantly straining to support all that unbalanced weight. No wonder so many of us are suffering from occasional neck, back, and shoulder pain. Placing a small slanted cushion that raises our buttocks slightly forward can help alleviate back pain.

Nutritional Supplements that have antiflammatory properties include: Tumeric, Yucca (a natural cortisone), MSM, Magnesium, Omega 3's , Bromelain, Pycnogenol, grape seed extract, Boswellia, fish oil, flax seed, and Ginger. Boswellia and

Ginger are especially helpful for fibromyalgia pain. Remember that supplements by themselves will never be as effective as dietary change and supplements.

Homeopathics can be helpful for pain. Rhus toxicodendron helps arthritis and fibromyalgia pain. Arnica montana is good for any kind of pain, especially muscular pain and has almost no side effects. Follow the directions on the bottle and let tablets dissolve under your tongue—do not chew them. Take homeopathics ten minutes away from food. You can take tablets every fifteen minutes for the first two hours, and then four times a day. It will usually work within the first week.

LYMPHASIZING

Improving lymphatic flow will help prevent muscle soreness and also strengthen the immune system. You may wish to consider a series of lymphatic massages by a therapist trained to move the lymphatic fluids and toxins out of the lymph system. This is done by stroking the hands in the direction of the lymphatic vessels without any downward movements and always toward the heart. Drink extra water after this type of massage. Speed up healing by using your own lymphatic massage with the following three methods:

1. Pressure
2. A massage motion
3. A light fast stroke

If you have a lot of pain use a light fast stroke as though were brushing dust from your shoulder, finger, knee, hip or wherever pain is located. If it is your finger and it too painful to hold, us a light fast stroke, wait 15 seconds, then try massage. Repeat the light fast stroke followed by massage before the pain comes back. You can also apply pressure with your fingers by pushing on each side of where the pain is located. Repeat these self-help pain techniques every 15 minutes to keep the excess fluid and acidic lactic acid out of the tissues.

If you could get all the generators turned on in the cells of your body, would you be healthy? According to Dr. C. Samuel West, the answer is "Yes." To do this, he recommends a basic lymphasizing program. The idea for the program came from Dr. Norman Walker.

Walker West Walk--Oxygenation

Walker had an exercise that could move the lymphatic system and helped remove trapped proteins. He named it the "Walker West Walk," and it is so simple, that anyone can do it. Children like to call it the Choo-Choo Train.

Exhale as deeply as you can, then using the "SHHH" sound, inhale as deeply as you can. Do this through your teeth. Inhale, exhale, inhale, exhale, exhale, exhale, completely emptying your lungs by the last exhale. Repeat this process over and over again. You may alternate by doing: Inhale, inhale, inhale, inhale, exhale, exhale, exhale, and exhale. Only do the first part once or twice because some of you may become dizzy or light-headed.

The second part involves swinging you arms and stepping lively along with the breathing exercise. If you can't do that yet, just sit down and swing your arms as you inhale, exhale, inhale, exhale. If you can do it, step as lively as you can while you swing your arms, but do not get tired or cause any negative stress on your body. The more you are able to do it, the better you will feel. You may need to do this gradually. Increase the number of times and the length of time you do this exercise as you feel like it. You will get more oxygen to the lungs and to the cells and your body will become more alkaline.

Dr. Stephen E. West, in his book, "The Golden Seven Plus Two," says lack of oxygen causes most pain. As you sit on a hard chair for a while, you will come to know this is true because it blocks circulation. Deep breathing is important. Also, as you move around the blood becomes more oxygenated and it helps take the pain way. Unhealthy cells contribute to fluid retention. That is why it is important to eat alkaline foods and avoid sugar, too much salt, bad fats and high cholesterol foods. Body fluids follow the blood proteins (acid). If we put too much water on a crop, we kill the crop.

These proteins must be removed by the lymphatics and we need movement to get the lymphatics moving. Doctors use electrical stimulators to help heal fractures, knees, etc.

Remember, the lymph system pumps fluid and proteins out of the tissue spaces each time the tissues are compressed or moved in some other way.

MOVEMENT- Mini Trampolines

Jumping on a trampoline is a form of lymphasizing. As you move up and down something magical begins to happen in your body. Research reveals that the lymph system pumps fluid and protein (acid) out of the tissue spaces each time the tissues are compressed or moved in any way. If you have a bad back, you may want to sit on a mini-trampoline and gently bounce. Consult your physical therapist or physician before beginning jumping on a mini tramp.

At the bottom of a bounce the one-way check valve closes. At the top, they open and the lymph fluids are propelled through the system, just like they are when you breathe in deeply. If you just walk around without breathing deeply at the same time, it is impossible to get the benefits of lymphasizing. If you can get the body to the aerobic zone (and some of you can't right now), you are breathing deeply and flooding the cells with oxygen which enables them to convert glucose into A.T.P. (adenosine triphosphate which helps transfer energy into the cells) and also into glycogen. The goal is to convert glucose into glycogen inside your muscle cells.

If you have a lot of toxins, start slowly and drink a lot of water after any type of exercise.

Chapter 10

FINDING PROFESSIONAL HELP
AND RESOURCES

*T*he tribulation of trying to find the right medical, holistic, or alternative health care help can be overwhelming and at times seem hopeless. My suggestion is to find a health professional who supports diet, nutrition, and who believes there is such a thing as candida.

The following are a few resources which I think may be helpful:. The International Coalition for the Advancement of Fibromyalgia & Fatigue treatment offers a DVD on their seminars, the latest in treatments and therapies for sufferers. Presenters are industry leaders and Dr. Jacob Teitelbaum. The web site is www.fibroandfatigue.com If it is still available they are offering discounted advance ordering of the seminar DVD Spotlighting the Latest in Treatments & Therapies for

Fibro & Fatigue" for only $19.95.. This site also lists a connection for locations and phone numbers for Fibromyalgia and Fatigue Centers across the nation.

I particularly like Dr. Teitelbaum because he knows CFS/FMS as an insider. He contracted the disease in 1975 when he was a student at the Ohio State University College of Medicine and had to take a leave of absence for a year to recover. In the ensuing years, he dedicated his career to, researching, developing and teaching about effective treatment and founded the Center for Effective CFIDS/Fibromyalgia Therapies in Annapolis, Maryland.

For over two decades, he has worked with Fibromyalgia and Chronic Fatigue patients and has a specialized practice for FM/CFS patients in Annapolis, Maryland. He continues to lecture to patient and physician/research groups internationally.

Dr. Teitelbaum is a board-certified internist and best-selling author. Dr. Teitelbaum joined Fibromyalgia and Fatigue Centers where he serves as Medical Director for the specialized treatment of Fibromyalgia and fatigue-related conditions. Dr. Teitelbuam's research and innovative approach led him to author a landmark study on effective treatment for Chronic Fatigue Syndrome/Fibromyalgia (CFS/FMS), which was published in the Journal of Chronic Fatigue Syndrome (8:2, 2001). This gold standard research showed an average improvement of 76% after 3 months of treatment, and a dramatic 90% average improvement after 2 years) using his comprehensive medical approach. Close to 50% of participants experienced a 133% increase in energy and a 58% reduction in pain after 3 months (see the study at www.endfatigue.com). Dr. Teitelbaum's work has also been editorialized in the Journal of the American Academy of Pain Management, in which his integrative treatment protocol was recognized as "standard of practice" for chronic pain conditions.

Dr. Elmer Cranton specializes in CFIDS/FMS at his clinic in Yelm, Washington, and has used nutrition and antifungal medications to successfully treat patients. He states his program would be termed unproven and anecdotal by most physicians because double-blind, placebo controlled studies have not been done. However, there have been clinical trials supporting this theory. A treatment program developed by Dr. Cranton to eliminate yeast from the body and to successfully treat CFIDS has helped hundreds of his patients who were previously unresponsive to other therapies.

Dr. Robert Young and his wife, Shelly offer a pH Miracle Retreat that is designed to be an enriching lifestyle experience filled with education and relaxation where you have direct access to Dr. Young and Shelley. The Young's will personally help you embrace the ALKALARIAN lifestyle.

It is located 50 minutes from the San Diego Airport in Pauma Valley on a hilltop site. It has lemon, avocado, and grapefruit trees, and an organic garden.

Amenities include a swimming pool, massage salon, walking trails and a tranquil and healing atmosphere.

The program includes:

Nutritional Consultation, culinary consultation, food prep and demonstrations with Shelley Redford. Luxury Lymphatic Hot Rocks Massage, exercise and rebounding demonstrations with Robert O. Young, D.Sc., Ph.D.

Nutritional supplements, Back to the House of Health 2 cook book, education and lectures, New Biology/Cycle of Balance. Fundamentals of Acid Based Chemistry. Seven Steps to ideal health and weight, product summary/Liquid cleanse, and presentations on Lymphatic System.

Call: 760-751-8321 or check the web site at: www.phmiracleliving.com.

Email address is: info@phmiracleliving.com.

Support Groups

Living with CFIDS requires adapting to an entirely new way of life. Because people with CFIDS often feel alone with their disease support groups can ease the transition for both the newly diagnosed patient and those who have had it for years. Support groups provide essential emotional support in the ongoing struggle with the disease. Knowing that others share this journey offers comfort, reassurance, and a great place to find out from others about treatments or diets that alleviate symptoms.

The major objective of a CFIDS support group is to provide a warm and caring environment where CFIDS patients can share their experiences and methods of living with a chronic illness. Sometimes the best words a CFIDS patient can hear is "I know how you feel" or "I understand" from someone who really does. Most CFIDS patients would agree that the greatest benefits a CFIDS support group offers are confirmation and validation of the illness and the assurance that they are not alone. Additionally, a support group can give members a greater sense of self-esteem and empowerment as they learn to cope and adapt to life with a chronic illness.

For additional information on support groups, please visit the following areas on the CFIDS Association's Web site at: http://cfids.org/resources/support-groups.asp.

The web site for the National Association of Fibromyalgia is: www.fmaware.org.

Chapter 11

OVERCOMING DEPRESSION
AND THE BLUES

You cannot keep the birds of sadness
from flying over your head, but you
can keep them from nesting in you hair."

L ike Jonah, we sometimes end up in the belly of the whale. At least that's what it feels like. If it's not the belly of the whale, maybe it's the blues, melancholy, or sadness. Some people feel temporarily blue because of loneliness, grief, death of a loved one, divorce, poor health, financial problems, or other life stressors. These moods usually lift and the person will function normally again, but if it lasts for more than several months and interferes with daily activities, professional help may be needed.

What causes depression? Depression can be caused by loss, feeling trapped, guilt, and anger turned in on yourself. Acknowledge your feelings; it's painful to lose a loved one in death or divorce. It's distressing to have health problems. Write about your feelings. Find a support group or someone you can talk to about your pain or loss, but don't dwell on it continuously. Widowed twice, I have felt the agony of loss and loneliness, but ultimately I had to ask myself, "How can I turn my pain into service or positive action?"

What are the symptoms of depression?

1. Poor appetite or overeating

2. Insomnia or inability to sleep

3. Low energy or fatigue

4. Loss of interest in pleasurable activities

5. Low self-esteem

6. Significant weight gain or weight loss

7. Poor concentration or difficulty in making decisions

8. Feelings of helplessness

9. Thoughts of suicide and wanting to die

10 Guilt; self-critical and blame yourself

11. Sadness

12. Loss of motivation

Measure Your Depression

On a scale of one to ten, where are you emotionally? Ten is good, one is bad and very depressed. If you are below a 3 or have thoughts of dying or suicide you need professional help. Almost every city has a free crisis line under the mental health pages in your phone directory. Talk to a friend, a doctor, go to the emergency room at your local hospital if needed, but get help.

Depression knocks at every door, but you don't have to invite it in as a permanent guest. Like my grandfather used to say, "Fresh fish and house guests shouldn't stay more than three days." If the blues stay more than a few weeks, someone needs to move, and exercise is a great beginning. Studies have shown that vigorous exercise stimulates circulation, produces an increase in endorphins and releases serotonins in the brain, the hormones that encourage contentment and cheerfulness. Aerobic exercises such as walking, jogging, swimming, dancing, jumping on a mini-tramp or bouncer, and biking can generate a significant antidepressant effect. Brisk walking is as effective as any other exercise.

A common misconception about exercise it that it will cause fatigue, but if approached sensibly for about twenty minutes a day, it can increase energy, alertness, and make you more relaxed. If you're not motivated, join an exercise group, a spa, or find a friend to walk with you. For those with physical limitations, chair exercises are available.

Say "Cheese!" University studies confirm that when we use our smile muscles and humor, it increases the endorphins in our brain. Humor is the ability to look at the absurdity in our own lives and find something to laugh about. It may not eliminate the problem, but it will help overcome the effect. Life is at least as funny as it is sad. Humor can stop misunderstandings and ease tension when no other strategies will work. Consider creating a humor folder with clever cartoons and quips. These clips are good to pass on to friends and family when they are ill, recuperating, or just need a chuckle to cheer them up.

While there are many causes of depression or the blues, good nutrition plays a vital role. My number one recommendation is to add essential fatty acids (EFA's) to your diet in the form of flax seed oil or a blend that contains both omega 3's and omega 6's such as marine/borage lipid combination. Omega 3's, raise the serotonin level in our brain, improve moods and are found in fresh deepwater fish, flax seed or flax oil. A good quality fish oil or evening primrose oil are examples of good fats. *Fats That Heal, Fats That Kill,* by Udo Erasmus is an excellent resource. Avoid saturated fat and transfatty acids. Bad fats (French fries, deep fried foods, etc.,) inhibit the synthesis of neurotransmitters by the brain because they cause the blood cells to become sticky and clump together, resulting in poor circulation, especially to the brain.

According to Dr. Norman Shealy, author of Alternative Medicine, and Dr. James F. Balch, author of Nutritional Healing, avoid sugar. That means honey, sucrose, dextrose, corn syrup, and fruit juice. Avoid drinks or foods with aspartame because it can block the formation of serotonin and also cause headaches and insomnia. Your body reacts more quickly to sugar than it does to complex carbohydrates. The quick increase in energy by the intake of sugar is quickly followed by fatigue and depression. Stevia is an excellent sugar substitute.

Candida is a major contributor to depression. As yeast multiplies in the intestinal tract, villi in the intestines is unable to absorb vital nutrients needed by the brain and body. You feel hungry, your body craves sugar and bread, which contributes to more yeast overgrowth. Dr. Crook's book is an excellent resource and has a candida questionnaire. The candida questionnaire can be pulled up on the internet at: http://cassia.org/candida.htm.

Remember when you are eating junk food, dead food without enzymes and empty calories, you are only feeding your mouth, not your body. Dead foods include food like coffee, sodas, candy, alcohol, pastries, peanuts, fried foods, processed foods, microwaved foods, and margarine. Live foods include foods like broccoli, avocados, spinach, celery, cucumbers, limes, lemons, fish, almonds, sunflower seeds, olive oil, grape seed oil, flax seed oil, tomatoes, onions, garlic, alfalfa, peppers, and sprouted wheat wraps. In the next minute your body is going to give birth to 720 million new cells. What quality of materials have you stockpiled in your body for it to use to make these new cells? When your body wears out, where are you going to live?

Our thoughts determine our feelings and actions. Wayne Dyer, a well known psychologist and author, has said, "When you realize that what you think about becomes your reality, you become very careful about what you think about." When an African shaman prays for rain, he prays, "Thanks for the taste of the rain. Thanks for the smell of the rain. Thanks for the rain," and somewhere out there it is raining.

We can change our thoughts and replace them with words from a positive song, positive affirmations, or appropriate music.

Worry is like a rocking chair, it gives us something to do, but it doesn't get us anywhere.

Helen Keller said,

"Keep your face to the sunshine and you cannot see the shadows."

It's normal to have a pity party when you are hurting, but make it a short pity party. My mother-in-law, Marie, was one of the most positive people I've known. She was in her 60's when first widowed, but said, "I'm not going to feel sorry for myself. I'll take myself to lunch or have friends over for dinner."

Marie frequently went for walks or to a shopping mall and said hello to everyone. She took lemonade out to the garbage man and in turn, he delivered her garbage can in the driveway next to her house. When Marie was nearly 80 she said, "I'm going to go visit the old people on the street." The old people on the street were in their 60's.

Keep a gratitude journal. Each day write down from five to ten things you are grateful for-laughter, the giggle of a baby, sunrises, sunset, trees, rivers, forests, mountains, blue sky, rain, flowers, the song of a bird, music, a healthy heart-the list could go on forever. Develop an attitude of gratitude. The chart is on the next page.

GRATITUDE JOURNAL

Date_____Prayer_____Meditation_____Exercise_____Service_____

_____
_____
_____

Positive Affirmation:

_____

Scripture___:_____
Other: _____
Humor: _____

Date_____Prayer_____Meditation_____Exercise_____Service_____

_____
_____
_____

Positive Affirmation:

_____

Scripture:_____
Other: _____
Humor: _____

Date_____Prayer_____Meditation_____Exercise_____Service_____

_____
_____
_____

Positive Affirmation:

_____

Scripture:_____
Other: _____
Humor: _____

Chapter 12

HEALING FROM THE HEART

*R*esearch confirms that our thoughts and emotions have a dynamic effect on our health and vitality. According to the HeartMath Research Institute in Boulder Creek, California, emotions are a product of the brain, heart and body acting in concert. The relatively new field of neurocardiology has firmly established that the heart is a sensory organ with a sophisticated information encoding and processing center or "heart brain." Its circuitry enables it to learn, remember, and make functional decisions independent of the cranial brain. We now know that the heart sends five thousand more messages to the brain than the brain sends to the heart.

This analysis of heart rhythms by an electrocardiogram (EGG) presents a powerful measure of neurocardiac function that reflects heart-brain interactions and autonomic nervous system , both of which are very sensitive to changes in emotional states.

Stress has a significant impact on health. Dr.Rollin McCraty, at the HeartMath Institute, and other researchers have found evidence that suggests there is an important link between emotions and the descending and ascending(neural signals, which flow from the heart and body to the brain) autonomic activity. According to McCraty, "These changes lead to dramatic changes in the pattern of the heart's rhythm. Specifically, we have found that during emotions such as anger, frustration, or anxiety, heart rhythms become more erratic and disordered. In contrast, sustained positive emotions, such as appreciation, love, or compassion, are associated with highly ordered or coherent patterns in the heart rhythms."

Extensive experimental data has been gathered documenting the role played by the messages from the heart in pain perception, hormone production, electrical cortical activity, and cognitive functions.

The heart, brain, nervous, and hormonal systems are fundamental components of a dynamic, interactive network that underlies the emergence of emotional experience. Many processes provide constant rhythmic input with which the brain is familiar—the heart's rhythmic activity, digestive, respiratory, and hormonal rhythms, and patterns of muscular tension, particularly facial expressions. This input is continually monitored by the brain and helps organize perception, feelings and behavior. These patterns form a stable reference pattern. When input is sufficiently different from the familiar reference pattern, feelings and emotions are generated and an adjustment must be made in an attempt to return to stability. One way to establish control is an outward action. For example, a confrontation at home with a family member may lead to feelings of anger which can prompt inappropriate behavior. We can make internal adjustments by self-managing our feelings in order to inhibit these responses. If we are not able to manage our emotions then feelings of anxiety, panic, hopelessness, annoyance, or depression will result. The following "Freeze Frame" technique is helpful in eliminating and dealing with stress. It is viewed as optimistic and hopeful.

Seven Steps to Eliminate Stress

While attending a convention for therapists, psychologists, and marriage counselors, I watched in amazement as about 75 professionals learned the following "Freeze Frame" technique.

At the beginning, some displayed symptoms of being stressed, anxious, overwhelmed, or other negative emotions or feelings. By using this technique, all lowered their stress level tremendously and some even overcame anxiety.

Repeating this exercise over and over as needed, changes the negative neural patterns in the brain. It leads to more effective communication, lowers blood pressure, improves decision making, helps students improve in school, develops better problem-solving skills, helps panic and releases obsessive compulsive tendencies. This strategy helps get rid of negative, stressful thought patterns and replaces them with more positive perceptions and emotions.

Steps:

1. When you are feeling stressed, have anxiety or panic, or are facing a problem, describe your feeling in one word. Examples could be anxious, fearful, afraid, confused, angry, frustrated, sad, disgusted, enraged, overwhelmed, lonely, victimized or depressed.

2. Now, shift your attention to the area around your heart. Imagine yourself breathing in through your heart- breathe in to the count of five, breathe out to the count of five. Continue doing this for several minutes.

3. Think of a positive feeling—the love you have for a child or grandchild. Try to experience that positive feeling and send that positive feeling or love out to someone else. You may want to think of a positive experience or place where you have felt serenity, peace or laughter. Work on recapturing that feeling right now.

4. Go back to step number two and again breathe in through your heart to the count of five and then breathe out to the count of five through your solar plexus while still experiencing the positive feelings.

5. Ask yourself what would be a good answer to your problem or a helpful attitude to balance and de-stress your mind and body. If possible, write it down. Heart perceptions and intuitions are often subtle. They gently suggest effective solutions for you and all concerned with the problem.

6. Sense any change to your original stress as noted in step number one. Write it down and sustain the positive feeling as long as you can.

7. Repeat these steps as often as needed.

Chapter 13

OPTIMISM:
HOW TO GET IT AND KEEP IT

"Far away there in the sunshine are my highest
aspirations. I may not reach them but I can look up and see
their beauty, believe in them, and try to follow them."

—Louisa May Alcott

W hen you can't change your situation you can change
your attitude and internal self talk. You can learn to be
an optimist rather than a pessimist. Long ago Epictetus wrote,
"Man is not disturbed by events, but by the view he takes of
them."

We are not born winners or losers, we are born choosers.
We are responsible for our own happiness. No one else can
make us happy. Our spouse, our parents, our friends and
family cannot make us happy. We create our own happiness
and sometimes "thinking makes it so."

> You cannot prevent the birds of sadness
> from flying over your head, but you can
> keep them from nesting in your hair.

Our emotions make a big difference in our mental and
physical health.

Seven Steps to Optimism
1. Say "Cheese!"
2. Express gratitude
3. Walk in the sunshine
4. Get rid of stinking-thinking
5. Optimism Chart
6. Exercise
7. Humor

Say "Cheese!" When you use your smile muscles, it changes the endorphins in your brain. University studies have shown that your brain can't tell the difference between a real or fake smile. One study indicates there is a unique pattern of activity in the brain when you laugh that helps combat physical and mental illness. Your body is more alkaline when you laugh.

Collect cartoons and jokes and put in a binder to give to friends who are ill or recovering or have suffered loss.

Laughter is the best medicine. We all need humor in our life.

Gratitude: Keep a gratitude journal. Each day write down five things you are grateful for.

Sunshine increases our serotonin levels which reduces pain and raises our endorphins and that makes us happier. Walk in the sunshine or use Blue Light Therapy.

Get rid of stinking-thinking. How we think determines how we feel, and how we feel often determines our actions. We can't afford the luxury of a single negative thought.

Do not allow ugly emotions to take place in your heart or your mind.

We can't think two thoughts at once so when you have a negative thought replace it with a happy song, affirmations, or just say, "I am a child of God on a divinely appointed earthly mission."

"When you realize that what you think about becomes your reality, you become very careful about what you think about."

—Wayne Dyer

Acknowledge your feelings.

Talk or write about feelings.

Keep a journal.

Don't awfulize.

If we lock ourselves in a jail of self-pity we are the jailers who hold the keys.

Forgive. When we harbor angry feelings toward another person, we are allowing them to live rent free in our heads. It can make you ill by harboring anger.

Anger raises cortisol which wears down the brain, raises blood pressure and leads to heart disease. Stress can be reduced by 50% by letting go of anger. Repeat this affirmation if you have a need to forgive someone.

"I am making a choice to forgive you. By doing so, I free myself from the bond I had with you through hatred, anger, resentment, or fear. I take my power back and gain the freedom that only forgiveness can bring. You cannot hurt me and you cannot control me.I forgive for myself."

The following page contains an Optimism Chart.

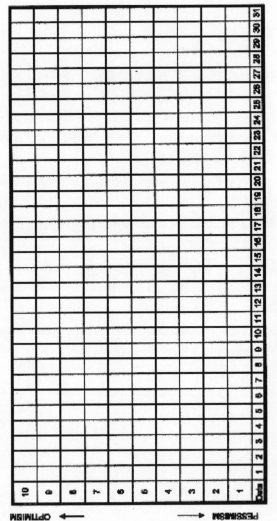

OPTIMISM CHART

MONTH _____

OPTIMISM ←

PESSIMISM →

	1	2	3	4	5	6	7	8	9	10	11	12	13	14	15	16	17	18	19	20	21	22	23	24	25	26	27	28	29	30	31
10																															
9																															
8																															
7																															
6																															
5																															
4																															
3																															
2																															
1																															
Date																															

INSTRUCTIONS - Imagine you are on an elevator with ten floors.

1. Find today's date.

2. Place an X on the floor level (between one and ten) above the date on the bottom row indicating where you think you are emotionally. If everything is going well and you are happy and content, place an X on floor 10. If you think things are going from bad to worse, place an X on floor one or the appropriate level. If you are somewhere in-between, place an X where you think you are emotionally.

3. Next decide what you can do to make things go better and what you can do to get to at least one level higher (from four to five for example)—maybe it will be small steps—be realistic; but plan to succeed.

4. Each day, explore ways you can climb to a higher floor or level and become more optimistic.

Patty Butts, Ph.D 2004

Look over the instructions on the previous page and copy the chart.

Imagine you are on an elevator with ten floors.

Ten represents very good and one represents awful.

Find today's date-place an "X" on your level of happiness, or emotional well-being.

Decide or brainstorm on what you can do each day to get to at least one level higher (from four to five).

Write down and explore ways you can become more optimistic.

Exercise What are exercises you do that relieves stress or makes you feel more optimistic?

> Walking
> Swimming
> Golfing
> Hiking
> Tai Chi
> Yoga

Humor

If at first you don't succeed, don't try sky diving.

Never trust a dog to watch your food.

Always wear a hat when feeding seagulls.

Chapter 14

WIN-WIN COMMUNICATION

A re you a doormat or a victim? Do you have trouble saying no, even when you should? Do you feel like a puppet on someone else's string? Are you bossy or a bully? Do you have little respect for the wants and needs of other people? Are you wishy-washy? Are you always getting in trouble with others?

If you answered "yes" to any of these questions, you may want to learn about assertiveness training.

Assertive behavior is the ability to honestly express your feelings, rights, opinions, thoughts, and beliefs in a direct way without trampling on the rights of others.

An assertive person is able to deal effectively with others without humiliating, dominating, or degrading the other person. They are able to express thoughts and feelings in a direct, open, honest and appropriate way in order to communicate expectations. She or he is able to make or deny requests such as saying "No."

Why is assertiveness important? Not being able to express our feelings or feeling like someone else is in control of our life causes considerable stress. Stress can be disastrous to our physical health and cause high blood pressure, headaches, ulcers and other symptoms.

If you don't know how to be assertive you might experience depression from anger that you turn inward, a sense of hopelessness or feeling helpless, with no control over your life. You may also feel resentment and anger at others for manipulating or taking advantage of you. It may come out as anger or violence. If you can't express anger appropriately, it can build up until it blows. Other feelings or problems can include anxiety or avoidance of situations that make you uncomfortable or frustrated at being a wimp or letting others victimize you. Non-assertive behavior leads to poor relationships and non-assertive people are sometimes unable to express emotions of any kind.

Parenting problems are easier when parents are assertive. Children are almost born knowing how to test the limits their parents set for them. If parents are not firm and assertive, their children will walk all over them.

To find out if you are assertive, aggressive, passive/aggressive, or passive circle the words that best describe you:

Aggressive: Dominating, bossy, rude, insisting, mean, harsh, pushy, explosive, thoughtless, superior, loud, overpowering, belittling.

Passive: Self-pitying, apologetic, victim, self-punishing, avoiding, giving in, giving up, withdrawn, injured, humiliated, doormat, timid, helpless, crying, sweet, no eye contact.

Passive/Aggressive: Resentful, spiteful, malicious, revengeful, malicious, two-faced, dishonest, bitter, condescending, sarcastic, fearful, gossipy, sulky, phony, late, grudgeful.

Assertive: Centered, negotiating, real, direct, clear, energized, competent, in control of self, powerful, aware, relaxed, considerate, flexible, listening, open, honest, responsible for self, moving.

Count the number of words you circled under each category. Are you aggressive, passive/aggressive, passive, or assertive? Because we do not always see ourselves objectively, have several friends or close family members circle the words they think best describe you and compare notes.

When we try to have a win-win relationship with a passive, passive/aggressive, aggressive person we are stuck and the relationship doesn't move forward. By the same token if we are anything but assertive we will have difficulty with all of our relationships.

I have counseled depressed women who seemed "sweet," but on the inside they were seething because their children or others took advantage of them. When I suggested assertiveness training or saying no to unreasonable requests their answer was, "I can't say no, people will think I am not nice or that I don't like them."

How do we become assertive? To become more assertive it is important to understand the language you use when communicating. "I" messages usually indicate an assertive focus and communicate that you take responsibility for what you think and feel. For example, "I really enjoyed attending the movie with you."

Using an "I" message is learning to focus your communication onto what you know about, rather than on what you assume others know about you. For example, "I felt really uncomfortable when you asked to borrow my car when all of our friends were present. I am not comfortable lending my car, but didn't want our friends to think I am selfish."

When you are assertive, the message is that although you and I may have our differences, we are equally entitled to express our opinions to one another without violating each other's rights. For example:

Stacy: "I am not comfortable attending another basketball game this week."

Dave: "This is the biggest game of the year and I really want to go."

Stacy: "Have you considered asking your brother to go with you?'

Dave: "Great idea, I'll call him."

This is flexible, win-win communication where both parties are open, honest and able to compromise. Another way to access the wants and needs of others is to measure them on a scale of one-to-ten. Ten is good, one is undesirable.

Dave: "On a scale of one to ten, where are you on going to an adventure movie tonight?"

Stacy: "I'm at a two, but I'm at a ten for hiking."

Dave: "I'm at a three for hiking. How about bowling?

Assertiveness does not guarantee winning, but it usually results in a compromise without making others feel angry.

"You" messages are normally aggressive and are directed to another person. These messages accuse, blame, judge or provoke another person. Messages such as "You should," "You will," "You must," "You can't," and "You ought to," are attempts to control the other person or situation by shifting responsibility away from the speaker onto the person being spoken to. For example, can you hear the blame in the statement "You never help me," or "You always mess things up for everyone."

When people are **aggressive** the underlying message is "I'm superior and always right and you are inferior. I am okay and you are not okay." Aggressive individuals make enemies. Their goal is to get some anger out of their system and dominate or humiliate others and they often do that by dominating and humiliating others.

"We" messages often have a **passive/aggressive** or manipulative focus. The speaker doesn't want to take responsibility and projects it onto others. For example: "We need to have a party for our teacher," or "We need to take care of the dog." "We really made a big mistake." "We should never do that." A passive/aggressive individual may be sugary sweet to your face, yet be vicious when you are not around. They are usually phony, two-faced, cynical, sarcastic, and vengeful. Their goal is to manipulate or use others to their advantage.

In contrast, **passive** individuals will withhold their wants, opinions and feelings. When you ask them what they want to do they will usually say, "I don't know." Passive individuals give up their rights and permit other people to "walk all over them." They are constantly apologizing and doing what they are told, even when they don't want to. Often they feel helpless, resentful and anxious. Passive people usually try to please others to avoid conflict or rejection.

Learning to be assertive takes practice. You may want to practice by having a conversation with yourself in a mirror or recording your conversation. You can have a friend or family member help you or take an assertiveness class in your community.

Remember that 75% to 80% of communication is nonverbal. Your tone of voice, body language, gestures, and posture are all part of your communication. Your tone of voice will either invite people into your space or stop them. If you are defensive, angry, hostile, or whiny, your message may not be heard. Even though your words may be assertive, if you're frowning, glaring, scowling, you're going to communicate anger. No one wants to be around a porcupine.

In refusing requests, don't apologize when you say no. This usually opens the door for more argument. For example, if a salesman is pressuring you to buy something you can't afford you simply say, "No, I'm going to find a car that is within my budget."

Sometimes you will find it necessary to refuse a request several times. This is frequently true of children or teenagers. If it is an important relationship you may want to acknowledge what the other person is feeling. "I know you were hoping that we could take a trip together and you may be disappointed, but I won't be able to go."

Three Parts of an Assertive Message:

A good assertive message communicates:

1. What you are feeling
2. Why you feel the way you do
3. What you would like to happen or change

For example: "I feel worried and anxious when you are late because I 'm concerned that something might have happened to you. I would like you to call me when you're going to be late so I know you are okay."

Avoid Victim Language

Do you use power or victim language?

Here are some examples of victim language. "My mother makes me angry." "If it weren't for my parents I would feel powerful." "I could be more independent and do what I choose if it weren't for my roommate." I'd be a lot more successful if it weren't for my childhood." " My friend makes me lose my temper." " I'd be more loving if my parents had given me more love." " I'd be happier if I lived in another city."

When we are assertive, we feel more self-confident and are better able to help others, but more than that, we have personal power in our own life.

Chapter 15

DEEP RELAXATION OR
SELF-HYPNOSIS FOR HEALING

*Y*ou may buy a relaxation or self-hypnosis tape or record the following instructions. allowing time for brief pauses. After you have finished your recording, find a comfortable place to sit or lie down. Do not worry if you fall asleep and do not operate the tape while driving. Press the button on the tape player.

Close your eyes, let your mouth drop open for a moment and move your jaw gently from side to side. Close your mouth slowly, keeping your teeth slightly apart. Take a deep breath.....Breathe in so that the air flows into your lungs and feels as though it's filling up your stomach area. Now, breathe out slowly....feel yourself floating down.

Focus your attention fully on your breathing. Imagine your breathing is as automatic as the ocean waves, rolling in......rolling out...in, out, in, out. As you breathe, feel the relaxation flowing over your body, one wave after another, down your shoulders, chest, into your arms, down your back muscles, down into your hips and legs. Feel the heaviness and warmth of your arms and legs.

Now find a spot on the ceiling or wall, just one tiny spot to focus on. Take a deep breathe and focus on that spot. You feel peaceful and relaxed. Count backwards from ten to one: Ten, nine, eight, seven, six, five, four, three, two, one. If you are not relaxed start over again counting backwards from 100.

As I become more relaxed, I realize I am taking control of my appetite and my life. Because I have more respect for myself and my body, I decide to eat only what my body needs.

I know that light, alkaline, green foods bring about a light, clear, clean body. I enjoy eating healthy foods and drinking water.

I eat salads and raw veggies and eat five or six small meals a day. I am full of satisfaction and am in control of my life.

I constantly see myself as the new healthy me, looking fit, healthy, slim, and in control. I hold this picture of the new healthy, energetic, positive me in my mind all the time, especially when getting up in the morning, just before going to bed at night and also just before eating food.

I am pleased with the way I see myself now and I look forward to the day when the new me merges with this positive picture in reality.

If there is ever a time when I think of food and know for sure that it is not appropriate at that time, I place my hand on my stomach and think to myself, "healthy body, slim figure." That immediately gives me a feeling of inner satisfaction so that I know I don't need to eat.

I enjoy having a sense of humor. Humor helps heal my body. I enjoy laughter.

Take a deep breathe and slowly return for the relaxation state.

Whenever you crave unhealthy food, place your hand on your stomach and say to yourself, 'HEALTHY BODY, MIND AND SPIRIT." Listen to the tape several times a day.

Chapter 16

HUMOR AS A HEALING TOOL

Laughter is not only the best medicine, it is the cheapest.

"*L*aughter is the sun that drives winter from the human face," said Victor Hugo. People need laughter sometimes more than food. Increasing your chuckles and laughter can be as important as taking your daily nutritional supplements.

Through humor, you can soften some of the worst blows that life delivers. Once you find laughter, you can survive even the most painful situations. Most chronic fatigue/FMS patients I have talked to have had some serious or multiple stressors prior to becoming ill. Acute stress is experienced in response to an immediate perceived threat, either physical, emotional or psychological. The threat can be real or imagined; it's the perception of threat that triggers the response.

Laughter reduces the level of stress hormones like cortisol, adrenaline, epinephrine and growth hormone. Stress hormones are usually released during the flight or fight response. The response was originally named for its ability to enable us to physically fight or run away when faced with danger, it's now activated in situations where neither response is appropriate, like in traffic or during a stressful day at work. When the perceived threat is gone, systems are designed to return to normal function via the relaxation response, but in our times of chronic stress this often doesn't happen enough, causing damage to the body.

Epinephrine is a naturally occurring hormone. When we are under stress or during the fight or flight response, the adrenal gland releases epinephrine into the blood stream along with other hormones like cortisol. They signal the heart to pump harder, increase blood pressure, opening airways in the lungs, narrowing blood vessels in the skin and intestine to increase blood flow to major muscle groups, and performing other functions to enable the body to fight or run when encountering a perceived threat.

Laughter increases the level of health-enhancing hormones like endorphins, and neurotransmitters like serotonin. Endorphins lift depression and alleviate pain. Serotonin helps us feel good and better cope with our challenges.

Laughter strengthens the muscles and bones, the respiratory system, the central nervous system, the cardiovascular system, enhances circulation, stimulates digestion, and oxygenates the blood. It also reduces stress and anxiety and makes your body more alkaline.

Laughter increases the number of antibody-producing cells and enhances the effectiveness of T cells. All this means a stronger immune system, as well as fewer physical effects of stress.

I like the story of the airline pilot...

A man was flying from Seattle to San Francisco. Unexpectedly, the plane was diverted to Sacramento along the way. The flight attendant explained that there would be a delay, and if the passengers wanted to get off the aircraft the plane would re-board in 50 minutes.

Everybody got off the plane except one lady who was blind. A man had noticed her as he walked by and could tell the lady was blind because her Seeing Eye dog lay quietly underneath the seat in front of her throughout the entire flight. He could also tell she had flown this very flight before because the pilot approached her, and calling her by name, said, "Kathy, we are in Sacramento for almost an hour. Would you like to get off and stretch your legs?"

The blind lady replied, "No thanks, but maybe my dog would like to stretch his legs."

Picture this:

All the people in the gate area came to a complete standstill when they looked up and saw the pilot, wearing sunglasses, walk off the plane with a Seeing Eye dog!

People immediately not only tried to change planes, but they were trying to change airlines!

Laughter is:

- **Physical Release:** Have you ever felt like "I have to laugh or I'll cry"? Have you experienced the cleansed feeling after a good laugh? Laughter provides a physical and emotional release.

- **Internal Workout:** A good belly laugh exercises the diaphragm, contracts the abdominal muscles and even works out the shoulders, leaving muscles more relaxed afterward. It even provides a good workout for the heart.

- **Distraction:** Laughter brings the focus away from anger, guilt, stress and negative emotions. Milton Berle said, "Laughter is an instant vacation."

- **Perspective:** Our response to stressful events can be altered by whether we view something as a "threat" or a "challenge." Humor can give us a more lighthearted perspective and help us view events as "challenges," thereby making them less threatening and more positive.

- **Social Benefits of Laughter:** Laughter connects us with others. Also, laughter is contagious, so if you bring more laughter into your life, you can most likely help others around you to laugh more, and realize these benefits as well. By elevating the mood of those around you, you can reduce their stress levels, and perhaps improve the quality of social interaction you experience with them, reducing your stress level even more!

Insanity is hereditary; we get it from our children. They also give the gift of laughter. Some incidents may not be funny at the time, but later bring a chuckle. Once I was rushing to attend a meeting, but could not find my pantyhose, and knew I had placed them on the bed. I rushed around looking all over the bedroom, then throughout the house searching and asking the children if they had seen my hose. No one had seen them. Finally, in desperation I decided to go bare-legged even though it was the middle of winter. While rushing for the door, three-year-old Jackie ran to give me a hug goodbye. As I picked her up, I looked at her surprisingly tan legs and the stockings dangling from her feet. She was wearing my pantyhose.

"Mirth is God's medicine. Everybody ought to bathe in it."
—Henry Ward Beecher

How To Use Laughter:

Pre-school-aged children laugh up to 400 times a day, but by the time we reach adulthood, we laugh a mere 17 times per day on average! Here is how to raise your laughter level with the following strategies:

- **Entertainment:** There's no shortage of comedies out there, both at the theater and in the aisles of the video stores, as well as right on your television. Watching something marginally funny may actually frustrate you, while watching truly hilarious movies and shows is an easy way to get laughter into your life whenever you need it.

- **Laugh With Friends:** Going to a movie or out to dinner with friends is a great way to get more laughter in your life. Laughter is contagious and the effects of laughter may mean you'll laugh more. Having friends over for a potluck party or game night is also a great setup for laughter and other good feelings.

- **Find Humor In Your Life:** Instead of complaining about life's frustrations, try to laugh about them. If something is so frustrating or depressing it's ridiculous, realize that you could "look back on it and laugh." Think of how it will sound as a story you could tell to your friends, and then see if you can laugh about it now. With this attitude, you may also find yourself being more light-hearted and silly, giving yourself and those around you more to laugh about. Approach life in a more mirthful way and you'll find you're less stressed about negative events, and you'll achieve the health benefits of laughter.

- **"Fake It Until You Make It:"** Just as studies show the positive effects of smiling occur whether the smile is fake or real, faked laughter also provides the benefits mentioned above. So smile more, and fake laughter; you'll still achieve positive effects, and the fake merriment may lead to real smiles and laughter. Say

"Cheese!" and use your smile muscles. The brain can't tell the difference between a real smile and a phony smile. This will raise your endorphins.

- **Look for the Absurd:** Keep an open mind for the outrageous, and the silly things in your own life. Hang out with children, they understand silly and laughter.
- **Relish the Sound of Your Own Laughter:** Record you own laughter, the laughter of children, or a someone else's that you really like.
- **Journaling with a Focus on Humor:** There is a therapeutic benefit of journal writing with a particular emphasis upon the healing potential of the humor and wit that emerges from writing. You can start anywhere--childhood experiences, family reunions, life on your street, apartment building, neighborhood, or relationships with family or neighbors. Just think back on some of the humorous things that have occurred.

Jack Handey, from *Saturday Night Live*, said "Dad always thought laughter was the best medicine, which I guess is why several of us died of tuberculosis."

May every parent be blessed with a sense of humor.

Somehow I survived the terrible two's of twins and made it to the awful three's. That's when the fun really began. One day, while in the shower, I heard the refrigerator door open and shut. *What now?* I wondered. Cutting the shower short, I wrapped a large bath towel around me and headed for the kitchen-on the floor was an empty egg carton and raw eggs all over. The twins were sliding back and forth in the jellied gooey mess. They giggled as they skated across the floor and wiped eggs on each other. Jackie had a fly swatter and kept hitting the yolks saying, "Gotcha!" Even their hair was covered in eggs.

I had thirty minutes before I was to teach a class for a group of young women. Saying a silent prayer, I filled the tub with bath water and dunked the girls in the tub, clothes and all. As I removed their mucky clothing, the babysitter arrived early. Prayers are answered.

A Test for Professionals

The following short quiz consists of four questions and will tell you whether you are qualified to be a professional. The questions are NOT difficult.

1. How do you put a giraffe into a refrigerator?

The correct answer is: Open the refrigerator, put in the giraffe, and close the door. This question tests whether you tend to do simple things in an overly complicated way.

2. How do you put an elephant into a refrigerator?

Did you say, Open the refrigerator, put in the elephant, and close the refrigerator? Wrong answer.

Correct Answer: Open the refrigerator, take out the giraffe, put in the elephant and close the door. This tests your ability to think through the repercussions of your previous actions.

3. The Lion King is hosting an animal conference. All of the animals attended except one. Which animal did not attend the conference?

Correct Answer: The Elephant. The elephant is in the refrigerator. Remember, you just put him in there. This tests your memory. Okay, even if you did not answer the first three questions correctly, you still have one more chance to show your true abilities.

4. There is a river you must cross but it is used by crocodiles, and you do not have a boat. How do you manage it?

Correct Answer: You jump into the river and swim across it. Have you not been listening to anything I've said? All of the crocodiles are attending the animal conference called by the Lion King. This tests whether you learn quickly from your previous mistakes.

According to Anderson Consulting Worldwide, around ninety (90%) percent of all professionals tested got all of the questions wrong, but many of the preschoolers tested got several correct answers. Anderson Consulting says this conclusively disproves the theory that most professionals have the brains of a four-year-old.

—Author Unknown

Chapter 17

AFFIRMATIONS

As a man thinketh in his heart, so is he. (Proverbs 23:7)

O ur Thoughts Determine Our Feelings and Actions

How we think determines how we feel, and how we feel often determines our actions. By developing positive self-talk, we can conquer our negative feelings.

The following are some affirmations that have been collected over the years. You can record these affirmations on tape, listen, write down, read, or say out loud any of these on a daily basis.

1. Healing and love flow through my body like a gentle breeze caressing my soul.

2. My mind and body are healing.

3. Nature is cleansing my body and mind, and I am assisting in the process.

4. I am a clear channel for positive thinking.

5. My body and spirit are in perfect alignment.

6. It is a wonderful day.

7. All things that are part of the divine plan of my creation now come into my life.

8. I am in communion with my higher power.

9. I have all the inner peace and tranquility I need.

10. My body and spirit are in perfect alignment.

11. I joyfully share my abundance with others.

12. My body nourishes me with love and light.

13. I have all the money I need to succeed.

14. I am a child of God, filling a divinely appointed earthly mission.

15. Abundance now flows into my life.

16. I enjoy being a positive thinker.

17. The universe is backing me up in all my obligations and decisions.

18. I am peaceful and serene.

19. My heart is open to joy and happiness.

20. I have a sense of humor.

21. I enjoy laughter.

22. My blood is abundant with life's energy.

23. I allow myself to experience the happiness and joys of life.

24. Laughing, humor and love are all positive parts of my life.

25. Prosperity now comes into my life.

26. I really like myself.

27. I freely forgive all people and embrace them.

28. I am calm, serene, and have peace of mind.

29. All my thoughts are loving and happy.

30. My positive thoughts give me strength, happiness and peace.

31. My life runs smoothly at all times.

32. Help and support are always available to me when I need them.

33. I have all of the positive power I need to take charge of

my life.

34. I enjoy serenity.

35. I can clearly see all of the beauty surrounding me.

36. I am overcoming all obstacles.

37. I am creating my own happiness; no one else can create it for me.

38. I am joyfully happy.

39. I have the energy, time, and wisdom to make my world a happy place.

40. I fill myself with love and light with each breath I take.

41. I enjoy a beautiful world.

42. I am releasing all the anger and frustration in my life.

43. I am now happily successful.

44. Each day I see myself becoming more successful.

45. I give myself the power and permission to be a success.

46. All things are working together for health, success and love in my life.

47. I am calm and have peace of mind.

48. My thoughts are loving and happy.

49. I freely forgive everyone who has ever offended or harmed me, beginning right now.

50. I see myself as a successful person.

51. I enjoy helping other people as I succeed.

52. I am now growing healthy in a totally new way.

53. I now balance my body, thoughts and feelings easily each day.

54. I am now renewing my body's ability to heal itself.

55. I freely release all pain, illness and imbalance.

56. I feel stronger each day.

57. My body grows more beautiful as life gives my health back to me.

58. I enjoy weighing my ideal weight.

Chapter 18

FACING FEARS

*P*eter McWillaims, in his book, *You Can't Afford the Luxury of a Single Negative Thought*, states that we should fear some things—drinking poisons, leaping off tall buildings, and situations in which our physical body is in danger of extinction. He says, "All other fears-the ones we face each day-are illusions. They should be given no more credence or authority over our actions than television commercials, election-year promises, or people who try to sell us flowers in airports."

Three things you should know about fear.

1. Fear is an illusion.
2. Fear is your negative self-talk.
3. You can conquer fear.

Dr. Wayne Dyer, a well known psychologist and author, says that what we think about comes into our life. If we think positive thoughts, positive results will come into our life. If we think negative, negative results will come to us. "When you realize that what you think about becomes your reality, you become very careful about what you think about."

On the other hand, what you haven't received from the universe or destiny (or whatever you want to call it)... may be because of our own apprehensions and aversions towards what we think we would like to receive (your goals, ambitions, dreams, etc.)

One way of getting rid of your self-made blocks is to release all the hidden trapped fears inside you. You may feel you are fearless... but... digging a bit deeper will bring you across many of your fears that you don't even realize are bottled up inside you.

Begin by writing down five fears.

1. Close your eyes. Take a deep breath. Breath out slowly while counting 5 to 1 in your head...

2. Repeat step (1) 3 - 5 times.

3. Pause.... Relax in the Now. Let all feelings, sensations, sounds etc, do whatever they are doing... Let Them Be... relax

4. Say to yourself, "Let anything I fear consciously or subconsciously come up."

5. Relax... don't go looking for the fear... the first of them should come up in less than 30 seconds.

6. Don't be afraid... it's just a bodily feeling.

7. Accept the fear and let it grow as much as it wants to within you. Say to yourself "I welcome this fear as best as I can"

8. Visualize yourself holding this fear and now release the fear from your hands as you say "I allow myself to let go of this fear forever."

9. Pause. Look inside you... if it is still there repeat step (8)

10. The fear will actually leave your system the VERY FIRST TIME, whether you feel or realize it or not.

11. Now Go Back to step (4) and repeat steps 4 through 11. For some of you, the released fear will make space for other emotions which have been locked and bottled up to come up. Simply go through steps 4 - 11 if you feel the new emotions automatically coming up. Remember emotion is not fear. If this is uncomfortable for you, repeat steps 4-10 replacing the word "fear" with "this new emotion."

You can also do steps 1 to 3 with your eyes open. Now write down what fears may be there inside you. Let the answers come to you, don't rush.

After writing down about 5 fears, look at the first fears you've written down and go to step 9. - "I allow myself to let go of this fear forever." After you are free from the first fear, look at your second fear, release it and continue until you release all of the fears listed.

The easier paced this exercise is - the better it will be.

If you are having a hard time getting in touch with your fears, here is a list of locked up fears that may serve as a trigger.

1. I fear Poverty
2. I fear having No Income
3. I fear Boredom
4. I fear Evenings
5. I fear Mondays
6. I fear Disapproval
7. I fear being surrounded by Selfish People
8. I fear Not Being Able To Find Serenity
9. I fear a Loveless Life
10. I fear Carrying Bitterness towards others will last the rest of my life
11. I fear Failure.
12. I feel being Backstabbed.
13. I fear being Lonely.
14. I fear Not Being Able to Succeed.
15. I fear Not Being Able to Control my Temper.

You may also go to Chapter 11, *Healing from the Heart*, and review the seven steps to eliminate stress. They also apply to eliminating, pain, fear, anxiety, and illness.

Rudyard Kipling wrote, "Of all the liars in the world, our fears are the greatest."

Chapter 19

CIRCADIAN RHYTHMS, SLEEP DISORDERS, INSOMNIA

M ost, if not all CFIDS/FMS patients have an associated sleep disorder such as alpha-EEG anomaly, insomnia, or sleep apnea. Alpha-EEG is characterized by the ability to fall asleep without much trouble, but the deep level of sleep is interrupted by bursts of awake-like brain activity. Patients seemed to spend the night with one foot in sleep and the other in wakefulness. Other patients deal with inability to fall asleep or early morning insomnia. Research suggests this may be due to the body clock or circadian rhythms.

Circadian Rhythms are our body's natural cycles that control appetite, energy, mood, sleep and libido. When our body is out of sync with nature, we suffer from a Circadian Rhythm Disorder. Almost all of us, at some time during a year fall out of balance and suffer from sleep, mood or anxiety disorders. Fortunately, after decades of research, science has found the way to create circadian balance.

Nature's Rhythms

Nature is made up of rhythms or cycles. Common rhythms include the four seasons and the twenty-four hour rotation of the earth. Like nature, our bodies have rhythms. Some of the rhythms of body and mind are tied to nature. When working properly, our bodies respond to nature's cues to create their ideal rhythms. For example, when functioning properly, the human circadian rhythm will respond to the morning light of a new day. This light will cue the body to produce cortisol, serotonin, and other hormones and neurotransmitters that get a person awake and going and cause blood pressure to increase and body temperature to rise.

At sunset, the body receives another of nature's cues and responds to dusk and ultimately the night's darkness. As the sun goes down the body will produce and secrete the hormone melatonin, and blood pressure will drop as the body prepares for and eventually falls off to sleep.

Circadian rhythms control the timing, quantity and quality of the hormones and neurotransmitters the body produces and eventually secretes. Hormones and neurotransmitters are the elements that determine how we feel, our sleep patterns, our appetite, our sex drive and other sleep and mood-related issues. When functioning properly, our circadian rhythms create circadian balance. When out of balance, quantity, quality and timing of hormone and neurotransmitter secretion suffer and our bodies suffer from a circadian rhythm disorder (CRD).

When I had Chronic Fatigue and FMS, I had great difficulty sleeping. It was a nightmare of insomnia, difficulty falling asleep, trouble staying asleep, waking at 3 or 4 a.m. in the morning and not being able to go back to sleep, and on occasion, sleeping from 12 to 16 hours and having difficulty waking up. This isn't unusual in CFIDS/FMS patients.

The Centers for Disease Control and Prevention (CDC) has documented that a circadian pattern exists in Chronic Fatigue Syndrome (CFS). Pain, fatigue, mood, social activity, energy, sleep and weight gain were significantly worse in the winter.

In addition, about half of CFS/FMS sufferers also have major depression in the winter. Circadian rhythms affect Chronic Fatigue and Fibromyalgia. Researchers have found success treating these patients with light therapy and have commented that, light therapy may provide patients with CFS/FMS an effective treatment alternative or adjunct to antidepressant drugs or sleeping pills.

The American Academy of Sleep Medicine estimates that at least 25% of all sleep problems are related to circadian sleep disorders. Other sleep problems are either caused by or contribute to circadian rhythm disorders. Circadian Rhythm Disorder (CDR) keep our bodies from enjoying a complete or rejuvenating sleep. Because CRD's disrupt the sleep pattern, they may contribute to narcolepsy, sleep apnea, snoring, and other sleep disorders. Most people find these symptoms diminish when their circadian rhythms are working properly.

What is a circadian rhythm?

All living things, are regulated by biological cycles, or biological events that repeat themselves at regular intervals. The rhythm of these cycles is called circadian, meaning spanning 24 hours. The sleep-wake cycle in humans obeys a circadian rhythm. These rhythms are the daily signals the body clock produces that tell us when to wake up, be energetic and go to sleep. CFIDS/FMS patients have body clocks that are not in sync with a 24 hour clock.

Researchers at the National Institute of Health found that using light at specific times of the day could re-entrain circadian rhythms to a normal pattern. Once body clocks were corrected, they would produce the necessary hormones at the right time of day, relieving the symptoms of sleep disorders and Seasonal Affective Disorder (SAD).

Bipolar Disorders—Hundreds of researchers have com

bined their efforts in a better understanding of how light affects CRD's that result in SAD, sleep, depression and related problems. Apollo Health has participated in many of these studies and has incorporated these results into its products, information and assessment tests. The light therapy equation developed by Apollo and its researchers will help sleep disorder SAD sufferers respond much quicker and better than with conventional light therapy.

Circadian Rhythm Disorders

An estimated 80 million North Americans suffer from some form of depressive mood or sleep disorder that stem from or are affected by a Circadian Rhythm Disorder (CRD). CRD disorders are manifested in the form of mood and sleep disorders such as:

1. Major Depression
2. Seasonal Affective Disorder (SAD)
3. Anxiety
4. Insomnia and sleep problems
5. Premenstrual Syndrome
6. Premenstrual Dysphoric Disorder
7. Mood Swings
8. Long or irregular menstrual problems
9. Menopause Disorders
10. Fatigue
11. Chronic Sleeplessness
12. ADD/ADHD
13. Prenatal Depression
14. Postpartum Depression
15. Fibromyalgia

Many CFIDS/FMS patients have some of these symptoms, especially, fatigue, chronic sleeplessness, depression, PMS, mood swings, and anxiety.

Numerous studies have shown that those suffering from FMS and CFIDS are deficient in serotonin, which is involved in the initiation of deep restorative sleep. "Serotonin helps regulate the perception of pain: the higher the serotonin level, the higher the pain threshold. Low serotonin and poor sleep can cause mental fatigue and confusion, known to FMS sufferers as "fibro fog." (Murphree, 2003, p. 16)

Mental functions, including rational thinking and short-term memory, begin to suffer when there are low serotonin levels. Normal brain activity decreases or even ceases when there is a deficiency in the chemicals (neurotransmitters/hormones) needed for proper function. (Murphree, 2003, p. 16)

Fortunately, after decades of research, science has found a way to create circadian balance. Significant research has been conducted to determine that those sufferers are dealing with a CRD. Research and clinical testing proves many sufferers can find relief from several common mood and sleep disorder's by correcting these rhythms.

Light therapy, also known as phototherapy, involves the use of light to stimulate the brain to produce neurotransmitters. You sit a few feet away from a special light box for a prescribed amount of time—usually up to 45 minutes every day. This light is stronger than ordinary office or household lighting. If light therapy works for you, your symptoms of insomnia and some depression will most likely improve significantly or disappear altogether.

Untreated disorders tend to become worse, not better. If you have a circadian rhythm disorder, your body is likely producing melatonin at the wrong time of day, when you need to be active. Studies have linked this maladaptation to higher cancer risks. CRD's may also contribute to stress and other health risks, since your body is not producing the hormones you need to be active and energetic. A recent nationwide study links higher mortality rates to insufficient sleep.

Our modern lifestyles demand more flexibility in schedules and man has lost touch with his most valuable tool to balance the circadian rhythm, which is the sun. Modern lifestyles, work schedules, and indoor living have altered the amount of sunlight we receive as well as how we set our schedules. It used to be that people generally woke up at dawn, worked and spent much of their day outside or near a window. This is no longer true.

What is circadian rhythm disorder?

When our bodies are out of balance nothing seems to feel right. This is because the hormones, chemicals and neuro-transmitters that determine how we feel, sleep and eat are out of sync. The result is a Circadian Rhythm Disorder.

A circadian rhythm disorder means your body is producing hormones, chemicals and neurotransmitters in the wrong amounts and/or at the wrong time of the day. Circadian rhythms stimulate the timing and production of countless hormones and chemicals that affect your sleep and mood. Circadian rhythms permeate practically every aspect of our lives because they so heavily influence the chemicals that determine our mood and sleep.

Nature, through its twenty-four hour cycle of day and night, has provided us with a template or a pattern that anticipates what we need to be healthy. Nature has obviously anticipated our needs and when properly synchronized, our bodies respond to nature's external cues.

Light is the most effective way to synchronize the body with the twenty-four hour day. Specific wavelengths, intensities and color spectrum of light, (not available in ordinary room lighting) can reset the circadian clock and create circadian balance. In addition to resetting the clock, light has a direct and positive impact by increasing brain serotonin levels. At the same time circadian light therapy has a depressing affect on daytime melatonin. Excessive daytime melatonin has also been linked to depression and sleep disorders.

A key point of the body clock or a region in the brain called Superchasimatic Nucleus (SCN) is its location in the human body. Because the SCN sits in the hypothalamus, it is connected to the optic nerve. When the eye is exposed to circadian light the SCN receives this signal and utilizes it as it regulates the circadian cycle. Unfortunately, most people no longer get enough daylight to receive the cues that nature intended and as a result there are millions of Americans suffering from some form of circadian rhythm disorder. Few of us get the amount of daylight needed. We live, work, and play primarily indoors. One study conducted in San Diego, one of the sunniest and ideal climates in the world found that people there received less than one hour of sunlight each day. The light they received was primarily to and from work while sitting in a car.

Check Your Circadian Rhythm

Apollo Health has developed a circadian rhythm assessment that will help you determine if you have a circadian rhythm disorder. Simply click on **www.apollohealth.com**, then click on circadian rhythm, then click on assessment, fill out the short questionnaire, and within several minutes it will pull up your assessment results. For example, I normally have a fairly stable circadian rhythm, but just recently have been waking up at 4 or 5 a.m. each morning. When I checked my rhythms the assessment determined that my I have an Advanced Circadian Rhythm Disorder (ACR) and my circadian rhythm is running faster than normal, causing me to produce the wrong hormones at the wrong time of the day. This causes lack of energy for me during the day, I tire too soon and awaken too quickly. By shifting my energy back to a normal cycle (as I have done in the past by using blue light therapy), I will experience increased energy with the ability to sleep better during the night.

Bright evening light, (using a goLite) has been shown to be the most effective treatment for ACR. Evening light slows the body clock down to a normal rhythm. This delays the onset of melatonin and sleep, allowing the person to sleep longer and have more energy in the late afternoon and evening.

Creating Circadian Balance

Circadian Balance is the state we enjoy when our bodies sleep well, eat right, have lots of energy and feel great; when in balance we are at our best.

Researchers at the National Institute of Health found that using light therapy at specific times of the day could re-entrain circadian rhythms to a normal pattern. They discovered that a very specific range of blue light is the most effective color (wavelength) in treating these disorders. Apollo Health has spent the last several years working with leading experts to develop an innovative line of BLUEWAVE products. Their goLITE delivers effective wavelengths, which means a more convenient treatment, and fewer side effects than traditional 10,000 lux full-spectrum light therapy devices.

BLUEWAVE (goLite) is the result of ten years of research with medical universities and the National Institutes of Health (NIH). Apollo has participated in this research and produce lights that are twice as effective at shifting circadian rhythms and suppressing melatonin when compared to 10,000 lux and white LEDs.*

After completing the Apollo Health assessment on your circadian rhythms, Apollo will give you a personal treatment schedule for using their goLite to balance your body clock.

In my case, for Advanced Circadian Rhythm Disorder, I began sitting to the side of the goLite (which was placed on my table where I could read) at 6:30 p.m. for 30 minutes for two evenings. The third night the time changed to 7 p.m for one night, and the fourth night at 7:30 p.m. for 30 minutes. This treatment continued for six days and by the end, my circadian rhythms were back to normal. The length and time will vary according to your assessment and what kind of sleep disorder you have.

I have successfully used the goLite to help a number of people balance their circadian rhythms. My neighbor hadn't had a good nights sleep in over two years. She checked her circadian rhythms, borrowed my GoLite for several days and for the past year she has slept peacefully. I have also used it with CFIDS/FMS patients who experienced improved results in sleep and mood.

Additional Suggestions for Insomnia

1. A lack of calcium and magnesium can cause you to wake up after a few hours and not be able to return to sleep so using these supplements may be helpful.

2. Take a hot bath (not a shower) an hour or two before bedtime. The drop in body temperature after a warm bath helps insomnia.

3. Sea salt or a few drops of an essential oil, such as lavender or chamomile can add to further relaxation. The scent of English lavender has long been used as a folk remedy to help people fall asleep. Now, research is starting to confirm lavender's sedative qualities. It's been found to lengthen total sleep time, increase deep sleep, and make people feel refreshed. Lavender appears to work better for women than men, possibly because women tend to have a more acute sense of smell. The good thing about lavender is that it begins to work quickly. Try putting a lavender sachet under your pillow or place one to two drops of lavender essential oil in a handkerchief.

4. Relaxation Techniques

Relaxation techniques are one of the most effective ways to increase sleep time, fall asleep faster, and feel more rested in the morning. They require a minimum of 20 minutes before going to bed. There are many different techniques:

Visualization involves imagining a relaxing scene. You can try it in bed before falling asleep. Involve all your senses. If you're imagining yourself on a tropical island, think of the way the warm breeze feels against your skin. Imagine the sweet scent of the flowers, look at the water and listen the waves-you get the picture. The more vivid the visualization and the more senses you involve, the more effective it will be.

5. Diet

Avoid stimulants especially in the evening or late afternoon.

Caffeine can have a pronounced effect on sleep, causing insomnia and restlessness. In addition to coffee, tea, and soft drinks, hidden sources of caffeine are also in chocolate, cough and cold medicine, and other over-the-counter medicine. Caffeine is also very acidic.

6. Avoid sweets

Although sugar can give a burst of energy, it's short-lived and can cause uneven blood sugar levels. This can disrupt sleep in the middle of the night as blood sugar levels fall.

7. Avoid the following foods close to bedtime: Cheese,
bacon, chocolate, eggplant, spinach, sausage, sugar, tomatoes, and wine. These foods contain tyramine, which increases the release of norephrinphrine, which is a brain stimulant.

8. Eat magnesium-rich foods

Magnesium is a natural sedative. Deficiency of magnesium

can result in difficulty sleeping, constipation, muscle tremors or cramps, anxiety, irritability, and pain. It has also been used for people with restless leg syndrome.

Foods rich in magnesium are legumes and seeds, dark leafy green vegetables, wheat bran, almonds, cashews, blackstrap molasses, brewer's yeast, and whole grains.

9. Lemon Balm was seen in ancient times as the ultimate remedy for a troubled nervous system, today it is known as both a sedative and stomach soother. The sedative action is attributed largely to a group of chemicals in the plant called terpenes. These occur in lemon balm in a unique combination that has earned the plant its reputation. It can also be given to relieve anxiety and nervous tension. It is a very good herb to counteract sleep problems.

10. Chamomile tea has been used for centuries as a natural remedy to calm and soothe. It is well known for its relaxing, sleep-inducing properties that help to alleviate insomnia, headaches and anxiety. In recent studies it was discovered that apigenin is one of the effective sedative compounds present in chamomile.

Although some natural practitioners recommend melatonin, according to some reports, more than occasional use can permanently stop the body's production of this vital hormone. In my case, when I tried melatonin, I experienced even more fatigue and a drowsiness the following morning.

11. For those with restless leg syndrome the homeopathic remedy Rhus Tox can be helpful. There are a number of homeopathic remedies available at your health food stores for insomnia and the good news is they have little to no side effects.

Chapter 20

ALKALINE RECIPES &
THE SHOPPING LIST

*T*he question I am asked most frequently is WHAT CAN I EAT?

The following is a shopping list of some foods that are alkaline:

Avocado

Asparagus

Cucumbers-one of the most alkaline foods you can eat.

Beets

Bell Peppers, red, green yellow

Broccoli

Brussel Sprouts

All kinds of cabbage

Carrots

Cauliflower

Celery

Chard

Romaine and Dark lettuces

Garlic

All Parsley

Jicama

Kale
Leeks
Lemons
Limes
Onion
Red potatoes
Spinach
Squash
Tomato
Water Cress
Zucchini
Almost any kind of fresh Herbs
Veggie Burgers (I buy the Morning Star Brand)
Veggie Crumbles (for casseroles or tacos)
Tofu (try to find tofu that isn't genetically engineered)
Manna Bread, Sun Seed or other varieties (health food stores)
Soy milk (Silk Brand is not genetically engineered)
Almond butter
Almond Milk
Rice Milk
Raw, unsalted nuts only
Almonds
Brazil Nuts
Flax seeds
Filberts
Pine nuts
Pumpkin Seeds
Sunflower Seeds
Sesame Seeds
Cereals
Amaranth

Basmati Brown Rice
Brown Rice Cakes
Buckwheat
Dulse Flakes
Kamut
Millet
Quinoa
Spelt
Use all kinds of spices
Flours
Spelt, millet, amaranth, kamut flours
Salmon and tuna can be eaten occasionally
Water
Distilled or reverse osmosis
Wild Rice

Vegan Menus
Breakfast—Choice of
- Soy Milk Smoothies
- Grapefruit
- Quinoa topped with avocados or broccol
- Cold cereal with rice, almond or soy milk
- Cooked millet, quinoa, or buckwheat cereal
- Scrambled Tofu
- Tofu burrito
- Quiche with tofu and soymilk
- Fried Tofu sandwich
- McTofu muffin with vegan ham

Some recipes can be found at this web site:
www.veganwold.com/recipes/

What to Munch for Lunch

Vegan Spreads

I like these spreads or toppings on Ezekiel Sprouted Tortillas or on brown rice crackers.

- Hummus
- TVP chicken salad
- Tofu egg salad
- Curried lentils
- Bean spreads
- Veggie Toppings
- Lettuce
- Tomato
- Shredded carrot
- alfalfa sprouts
- Peppers
- Red or yellow Onions
- Cucumbers
- Artichoke hearts
- Sundries tomatoes
- Black olives
- Coleslaw
- Ezekiel Sprouted Tortillas
- Veggie Burgers
- Vegetarian Cheese toasted on Ezekiel tortilla

Vegan Soups
- Vegetable
- Veggie Chili
- Noodle

- Cabbage
- Sweet/sour
- Split pea
- Black eyed pea
- Carrot Ginger
- Curry
- Barley
- Black Bean
- Potato garlic
- Wild Rice
- Lentil
- Spicy oriental
- Minestrone
- "Cream" of Broccoli

Vegan Salads
- Tossed salad
- Caesar
- Greek olive
- 3 bean salad
- Broccoli/sunflower/Baco
- BLT salad
- Cold asparagus salad
- Corn/bean salad
- Coleslaw
- Oriental Cole slaw
- Coleslaw with raisins/apples
- Copper penny salad
- Carrot Pineapple
- Gazpacho
- Cran-raisin spinach

Vegan Dinner

Use just vegetables or add Tofu or meat analogs in place of meat in any recipe

- Pizza no cheese
- Baked Potato with veggies
- Ready Made dinners
- Crispy Tofu nuggets
- Mexican
- Refried Beans
- Fajitas with veggies
- Burritos
- Beans/rice/veggies
- Oriental Over Rice or Noodles
- Chop Suey
- Beefy broccoli
- "Beef" and bokchoy
- Chinese "Chicken" and Veggies
- Sweet & sour
- Chow Mien
- Teriyaki
- Stir fried veggies
- Fried Rice
- Peanut Butter noodles
- Spicy Noodles with Cabbage
- Pad Thai
- Fried Tofu
- Cashew/ broccoli
- Sushi Rolls
- Pepper Steak
- Asian Asparagus Pasta

Pasta

- Spaghetti with red sauce (marinara) or vegetable sauce (primavera)
- Pesto
- Pasta With Broccoli
- Cajun Blackened Tofu Stroganoff
- Sun dried Tomato
- Vegan Alfredo
- Artichoke
- Lasagna
- Spinach
- Pine nuts

Vegan Recipes

Basmati Brown Rice with Tomato & Basil

1 cup Basmati brown rice
1 teaspoon sea salt
¼ cup lemon juice
1 packet Stevia
1 tablespoon good olive oil
Freshly ground black pepper
1 pound ripe tomatoes, large-diced
1 cup packed basil leaves (1 large bunch), chopped

Bring 2-1/4 cups water to a boil and add the rice and 1 teaspoon of salt. Return to a boil, cover, and simmer for 30 to 40 minutes, until the rice is tender and all the water is absorbed. Transfer the rice to a bowl.

Whisk together the lemon juice, Stevia, olive oil, ½ teaspoon of salt, and a pinch of pepper. Pour over the rice. Add the tomatoes and basil. Mix well and check the seasonings. Tofu or veggie crumbles may be added to this. Serve at room temperature.

Scrambled Tofu
3 T oil
1 sm. onion, chopped
½ red or green bell pepper, chopped
other vegetables-broccoli, carrots, potatoes, tomatoes, kale, etc., cut small
2 + cloves garlic, minced
1 # silken soft TOFU
2 heaping T Frontier Brand Beefy Broth Powder
1 t turmeric
Salt and pepper to taste

     Add onions, peppers, broccoli, and carrots.
     Sauté till thickest veggies are nearly cooked through.
     Add garlic and pepper, then tofu and remaining ingredients

Chilled Avocado Cucumber Soup - Serves 4
1 English cucumber, peeled and diced
(¼ cup reserved for garnish)
1 Avocado, pitted, peeled, and diced
½ teaspoon finely grated lemon zest, plus
1 tablespoon fresh lemon juice
¼ cup coarsely chopped fresh cilantro, plus sprigs for garnish
1 scallion, white and pale-green parts only, coarsely chopped (about 2 tablespoons)
1 jalapeño, seeded and coarsely chopped

1 cup of pureed coconut meat
1 cup of water
½ teaspoon salt
¼ teaspoon of Spice Hunter Zip

Puree ingredients in a blender. Divide soup and reserved cucumber and avocado among 4 bowls. Cover with plastic wrap. Refrigerate 30 minutes. Garnish with cilantro sprigs.

Pasta with Greens
½ cup sun dried tomatoes
1 pound dried whole wheat pasta (penne, rigatoni, twists, etc.)
1 pound greens (collards, kale, beet greens, chard etc)
2 Tbsp olive oil
1 large onion, thinly sliced
½ tsp hot red pepper flakes
2 - 4 cloves garlic, minced
1 Tbsp dried basil

Soak the sun dried tomatoes in hot water until soft, about 10 minutes.

Drain, cut into pieces, and reserve.

Begin cooking pasta according to package directions. While pasta is cooking, prepare greens by washing, removing all coarse stems and midribs, then chop coarsely and reserve.

Heat the oil (or water) in a skillet, add onion and red pepper flakes, and sauté over med high heat.

When onion begins to lose color, add the tomatoes and chopped greens, tossing well to wilt. Mash in the garlic, add basil, and cook for 5 minutes. Drain the pasta and mix with vegetables. Serve.

Dilly Ranch Dressing
1 cup Vegenaise
1 tsp onion powder
½ tsp garlic powder
1 tsp dried dill weed
1 Tbsp or lemon juice
Mix together well and serve.

Janna's Vegan French Onion Dip
 Place in a Vita Mix or food processor:
1 cup water plus 2 ice cubes
1 cup raw soaked almonds
¾ cup raw cashews
1 tsp garlic granules or bits (not powder)
2 Tbsp onion granules or bits (not powder)
1 1/2 tsp Real Salt
5- 6 Tbsp lemon juice
2 - 3 Tbsp Braggs Liquid Aminos
1 medium clove garlic, pressed
2 green onions
3 dates

Puree until smooth and creamy. Mix with 1/4 to 1/2 cup onion flakes or bits. Chill and serve with crackers or veggies.

Best of the Border Bean Dip
In food processor puree:
3 green onions, chopped
2 cloves garlic
1 Tbsp lime juice
1 Tbsp chili powder

1 tsp cumin
1/2 tsp Real Salt
1/4 tsp cayenne
Add to food processor:
1 can each: kidney, garbanzo, pinto beans
1 can green chilies
1 cup salsa

Pulse until mixed well but beans are still a bit chunky. It's also good completely pureed.

Spread 1/2 bean mixture on bottom of casserole dish.

Spread vegan sour cream 1/4 inch thick over beans.

Drop spoonfuls of remaining bean dip over sour cream. Spread carefully to cover.

Top with a layer of guacamole and garnish with black olives, tomatoes and sour cream.

Basmati Rice Dressing

Prep and cook time: About 1-1/2 hours
Servings: 10 - 12 (You can divide in half)
Notes: You can prepare this dressing through step 4 up to 1 day ahead; cover and chill. To reheat, let dressing stand at room temperature for 1 hour, then bake, covered, in a 350 degree oven until hot, about an hour.

2 cups brown basmati rice
1 cup dried sweetened cranberries
1 cup dried flaked coconut
2 cups slivered almonds
3/4 cup butter (I recommend Earth Balance)
2 cups chopped onion
1/2 cup chopped red bell pepper
1/2 cup chopped green bell pepper

2 tsp grated fresh ginger
2 tsp minced garlic
2 tsp curry powder
2 tsp ground cumin
2 tsp salt
1 tsp pepper
1 tsp ground cardamom
1 tsp grated orange peel
1 tsp grated lime peel
1/2 tsp ground cinnamon

Preheat oven to 350. In a 2-1/2 quart pan over high heat, bring 3-1/2 cups water and rice to a boil. Reduce heat to low, cover, and simmer until water is absorbed and rice is tender to bite, about 45 minutes.

Meanwhile, in a bowl, cover dried cranberries with boiling water and let stand until fruit is plump, about 15 minutes. Drain. Place coconut and almonds in two separate 10" x 13" baking pans. Bake, stirring occasion- ally, until golden, 4-5 minutes for coconut, 8-10 minutes for almonds. Melt butter in a 6-8 quart pan over me- dium high heat. Add onion, red and green bell pepper and stir until onion is limp, about 5 minutes. Reduce heat to medium and add ginger, garlic, curry powder, cumin, salt, pepper, cardamom, orange peel, lime peel, and cinnamon. Stir just until spices are aromatic-about 30 seconds.

Remove from heat. Stir in cooked rice, dried fruit, almonds, and coconut. Spoon into shallow 3-quart baking dish and cover with foil. Bake until hot in the center, about 30 minutes.

Vegan Chili - Serves 2-4
1 package Romaine lettuce
1 cup olive oil
½ onion chopped
1 whole jalapeno (seeds and all) You can used canned
chopped jalapeno
1 Tbs. Chili powder
1 tsp Real Salt
2 Cloves garlic, chopped
3 cups strained tomatoes (Pomi brand has no preserva-
tives or vinegar)
2 cups Salad mix (mixed greens, peppers, carrots etc)
Veggies shreds (cheese alternative) You can add a can
of black beans or kidney beans.

Brown in the olive oil in a saucepan or cast iron pot.
Add all remaining ingredients except salad. Adjust
seasonings to your own taste. If you don't like it too hot,
you can seed your jalapeno. Put about half of the chili in
a blender and add salad mix and puree. Pour back into
your pan, stir thoroughly. Pour into serving bowls and
top with alternative cheese shreds.

Kale Wraps
Large Ezekiel 4:9 sprouted grain tortillas
Dijon mustard
steamed kale
garlic granules
diced fresh tomatoes
grated carrot
minced fresh onion
thin slices of avocado
Lay tortillas out flat and spread with a thin layer of

mustard.

Then layer with steamed kale and sprinkle lightly with garlic granules. Top with tomatoes, carrot, onion, and avocado. Roll up tightly. Eat like a burrito or cut in slices and serve as an appetizer.

Hold the slices together with toothpicks.

Green Beans & Mustard

½ lb thin green beans, trimmed
1 tablespoon olive oil
2 tablespoons packaged unsweetened coconut flakes (preferably large)
½ teaspoon mustard seeds

Cook beans in a 3-quart saucepan of boiling salted water until crisp-tender, about 3 minutes, then drain in a colander. Rinse under cold running water to stop cooking and drain well. Heat 1/2 tablespoon oil in a 10-inch heavy skillet over moderately high heat until hot, then cook coconut, stirring, until golden, about 2 minutes. With a slotted spoon transfer to paper towels to drain. Cook mustard seeds in remaining ½ tablespoon oil over moderately high heat in a covered, shaking skillet until popping subsides, about 1 minute. Add beans to skillet with salt to taste and sauté, stirring occasionally until heated through. Serve, sprinkled with coconut.

Beans, coconut, and mustard seeds may be prepared separately 2 hours ahead and kept at room temperature. Sauté beans with mustard seeds and sprinkle with coconut just before serving.

Spicy Bean Burgers

1 Tbsp olive oil or water
1 small onion, finely chopped
2 garlic cloves, finely chopped
1 small green pepper finely chopped
4 oz frozen chopped spinach, thawed
14 oz cannelloni beans
¼ - ½ cup oats
1 tsp cumin
1 Tbsp chopped fresh cilantro
salt and pepper to taste

Heat the oil or water in a small saucepan and cook onion and garlic for 5 minutes until softened. Squeeze the excess moisture out of the spinach and place in a large bowl. Mash the beans well and mix with the spinach, oats, cumin and cilantro. Add fried onion mixture and stir well together. Season to taste and shape into four round burgers. Pan fry until golden brown on each side. You can cook these in the oven at 350o for 20-30 minutes. Serve on buns with all the trimmings.

Mediterranean Pasta and Garbanzo Bean Salad

4 cups uncooked rotini pasta
1/3 cup lemon juice
¼ - ½ cup olive oil
2 Tbsp minced fresh parsley
1 Tbsp Dijon Mustard
2 Tbsp minced fresh mint leaves
1 Tbsp dried oregano
1 tsp dried thyme

¼ tsp salt
½ tsp pepper
15 oz can garbanzo beans, drained
6-8 pepperoncini, chopped
4 plum tomatoes, diced
4-6 scallions, diced

Cook pasta in boiling water.

Drain; cool under cold running water. In large bowl, whisk together ingredients lemon through pepper. Add cooked pasta and remaining ingredients. Mix well and chill for at least an hour before serving. Serves 8.

Split Pea Soup

2 cups green split peas
¼ cup barley
8 cups water
1 onion, chopped finely
2 bay leaves
1 tsp celery seed
2 cups vegetable broth
(or ¼ cup Braggs and 1 3/4 cups water)
3 carrots, chopped
3 red potatoes, chunked
3 stalks celery, chopped
2 Tbsp parsley flakes
1 tsp dried basil
1 tsp dried paprika
1 tsp dried thyme
1/8 tsp white pepper

Place split peas, barley and water in a large pot.

Bring to boil, reduce heat and add bay leaves and celery. Cover and cook over low heat for 1 hour. Add remaining ingredients and cook for an additional hour or until vegetables are soft.

VEGGIE BURGERS

These burgers have a great meat-like texture. Barley is higher in protein than rice or other grains, and is a great fiber additive to any diet. Choose different seasonings to make these burgers the flavor you like.

2 C. steamed barley (cook like you do rice)
1 C. nuts (any raw shelled nuts: almonds, pine nuts, walnuts, pecans, macadamia nuts or sunflower seeds).
1/3 cup flax seeds. Grind in a coffee grinder
2 zucchini
3 onions
2 tomatoes
4 carrots
2 clove garlic
2 cups sprouted wheat tortilla crumbs (dry and grind in Vita Mix to flour)
1 C Veggie Broth-Pacific Brand
2 TB. dried herbs of choice (Spice Hunter has several good blends) OR 3 TB fresh herbs of choice
1 tsp. Real Salt

Put barley, veggie broth and ground flax seed in a bowl, stir together. peel and chop veggies (can be shredded in food processor if desired)

Combine all ingredients, mix well, and divide into portions to make patties. Form into patties and arrange on an oiled cookie sheet. Bake at 225 until brown on both sides (turn over 1/2 way through baking). Serve hot, or crumble over a salad cold.

Chickpea Veggie Salad-Serves 8
2 cups cooked Basmati brown rice
2 cups broccoli florets
3 medium carrots
1 medium zucchini
1 medium yellow squash
1 medium red onion
2 cloves garlic
1 15-ounce can garbanzo beans (chickpeas), no or low salt, drained
2 tablespoon lemon juice
2 teaspoons extra-virgin cold pressed olive oil
mixed baby greens

Cook rice according to package directions.

Chop broccoli, carrots, zucchini, squash, onion, and garlic in small pieces. To do this quickly and easily you may use a food processor with the S blade in place, by using the pulse setting so that the veggies aren't over processed.

Place chickpeas and rice in a bowl and mix in veggies. Add lemon juice and olive oil and toss to mix thoroughly. Place greens on a plate and top with the chickpea/veggie mixture.

Tahini and Cashew Cream Dressing
Blend in a blender:
½ cup Tahini (Sesame seed paste)
½ cup cashews
juice of 1 lemon
2 Tbsp maple syrup or agave nectar
4 Tbsp lemon juice
4 Tbsp soy sauce or Braggs Liquid Aminos

Water to blend to a creamy pourable consistency. When you take it out of the refrigerator the next day it will need more water. (I use this in place of oil or mayo in salad recipes)

The combination of seeds, beans, and greens is a high quality, easily digestible protein combination!

Rotini with Spinach, Chickpeas and Tomatoes
10 oz pkg. rotini
2 - 3 garlic cloves
1 can chickpeas (garbanzo beans)
1 can Italian style diced tomatoes
1 tsp oregano
1/4 tsp dried hot pepper to taste
10 oz fresh spinach

Begin cooking pasta. Sauté crushed garlic in a small amount of oil or water until browned. Add tomatoes, chickpeas, and remaining ingredients. Cook until hot. Stir in spinach, take off burner, cover and let sit for 5 minutes or until wilted. Mix with pasta and serve.

Enchilada Casserole

1 onion chopped
1 green bell pepper chopped
2 cloves garlic minced or pressed
1-1/2 - 2 tsp chili powder
1 tsp cumin
½ tsp coriander

Sauté' onion garlic, and peppers in water or Braggs Liquid Aminos until onions are transparent. Stir in spices then add:

1 4 oz can green chile's
4 cups cooked black beans
14oz can chopped Mexican-style tomatoes with juice
½ cup fresh chopped cilantro

Cook until heated through. Pour 1 large can enchilada sauce in flat bottom bowl or pan.

Dip tortillas in sauce and cover liberally. Layer in bottom of 9" x 13" pan. You may need to cut tortillas so they fit the pan. Spoon in ½ the black bean mixture and spread evenly over tortillas. Dip more tortillas in sauce and layer over bean mixture. Add the remaining beans and spread evenly. Top with more sauced tortillas and sliced olives.

REFERENCES

Alternative Medicine, (1997) compiled by the Burton Golberg Group. Future Medicine Publishing, Inc., Tiburon, Calif.

Balch, P., Balch, J. (2000). *Prescription for Nutritional Healing.* New York: Penguin Putnam Inc.

Bell, D. (1995). *The Doctor's Guide To Chronic Fatigue Syndrome.* New York: Da Capo Press, member or Perseus Books Group.

Brown, S. and Jaffe, R. "Acid-Alkaline Balance and Its Effect on Bone Health': *International Journal of Integrative Medicine,* Vol. 2, No.6, Nov/Dec 2000.

Brown, S. (1996), *Better Bones, Better Body*, New Canaan, CT: Keats Publishing, Inc.

Campbell, T.C., Campbell, T, (2005) *The China Study*, Dallas, Texas, BenBella Books.

CFIDS Chronicle, Fall 2004

Cousens, G., *Rainbow Green Live Food Cuisine, 2003*, Berkeley, Calif., North Atlantic Books.

Crook, WG. (1995) *The Yeast Connection and the Woman.* Jackson, TN, Professional Books.

Crook, WG. (1996) *The Yeast Connection Handbook*. Jackson, TN, Professional Books.

Crook, W.G.: "Yeast-connected immune system disorders: A commonly and usually unrecognized cause of chronic illness." *Journal of Holistic Medicine*. 1984; 6 (1) 38-40.

Cranton, EM.: www.drcranton.com/CFIDS.htm, 2005. Mount Rainer Clinic, Yelm, Washington, Mount Rogers Clinic, Trout Dale, Virginia.

Webb, Pat, *Defeating Depression & Beating the Blues*, Horizon/Cedar Fort, Springville,Ut

Endometriosis Association, 8585 N. 76th Place, Milwaukee, WI., 53223.

Goldstein, JA,: *Tuning the Brain: principles and practice of neurosomatic medicine*. 2004, Binghamton, NY, The Haworth Press.

Murphree, R. H., (2003) *Treating and Beating Fibromyalgia and Chronic Fatigue Syndrome*, Alabama: Harrison and Hampton Publishing.

www.niaid.nih.gov/factsheets/cfs.htm, May 2004.

Schmidt, M, Smith, L., Sehnert, K, :*Beyond Antibiotics*, 1994, Berkeley, Calif., North Atlantic Books.

Teitelbaum, J.: *From Fatigued To Fantastic: A proven program to regain vibrant health-- based on a new scientific study showing effective treatment for Chronic Fatigue and fibromyalgia.* Garden City Park, NY. Avery Pub. Group, 1996.

Truss, C.O.: "Restoration of immunologic competence to Candida albicans." *The Journal of Orthomolecular Psychiatry.* 1980. 9 (4):287-301.

Truss, C.O., *The Missing Diagnosis*, Birmingham, Alabama, 1993.

Truss, C. O.: "The role of Candida albicans in human illness." *The Journal of Orthomolecular Psychiatry.* 1981: 10 (4):228-238.

Truss, C.O, "Tissue injury induced by Candida albicans: Mental and neurological manifestations." *The Journal of Orthomolecular Psychiatry.* 1981.

Young, R. (2002). *The pH Miracle.* New York: Warner Books

Young, R. (2001). *Sick and Tired?* Utah: Woodland Publishing

Young, R. (2004) *The pH Miracle for Diabetes, A Revolutionary Diet for Type I and Type II Diabetes.* New York: Warner Book Publishing.

INDEX

A

acid, 4, 9, 10, 17, 21, 24-27,
36, 37, 39, 51, 60, 64,
68-70, 76
acidosis, 25-27, 37
affirmations, 84, 92, 113
alkaline, 9, 13, 21, 23,
26-28, 37, 45-49, 64,
69, 92, 104, 106, 133,
153
alkaline diet, 9, 13, 21, 28,
37, 46-49
allergies, 60
antibiotics, 4, 19, 20, 60,
154
antidepressants, 56
antioxidants, 28
anxiety, 60, 64, 88, 89, 98,
106, 119, 121, 124,
125, 131
assertive message, 102

B

balance, 9, 21, 23, 36, 41,
55, 76, 90, 115, 121,
122, 125-129, 143,
153
Balch, Dr. James, 61, 83,
153
Bell, Dr. David, 25, 28, 133,
140, 144, 152, 153
Beyond Antibiotics, 154
bloating, 10, 11, 17, 21, 60,
61
bowel, 10, 11, 21, 52, 59-62
Brown, S. And R. Brown,
24, 26, 27, 36, 37, 61,
135, 136, 139, 143,
145, 147, 150, 153

C

Campbell, Dr. T. Colin, 9,
31-33, 153
candida, 9-11, 2, 4, 10,
15-21, 24, 43, 48, 49,
51, 52, 61, 73, 83, 155
CFIDS, 9, 11, 6, 7, 9, 12, 13,
15, 17, 18, 20, 21, 24,
25, 45, 46, 48, 49, 53,
74-77, 121-125, 129,
153, 154
Chronic Fatigue, 3, 7, 9, 13,

1, 5, 9, 12, 15, 18, 20,
28, 54, 74, 105, 122,
123, 153-155
circadian rhythms,
121-123, 126, 128,
129
cloves, 11, 140-142, 145,
147, 150-152
colon, 41, 59, 60
communication, 89, 97,
99-101
corn syrup, 35, 83
Cranton, Dr. Elmer, 75, 154
Crook, Dr. William, 61,
153, 154

D

depression, 10, 49, 55, 57,
60, 79-83, 88, 98,
106, 123-125, 127,
154
Dyer, Dr. Wayne, 84, 93,
117

E

energy, 2, 4, 5, 7, 12, 13, 19,
23, 26, 28, 39-41, 46,
49, 52, 53, 71, 75, 80,
81, 83, 114, 115, 121,
122, 128, 130

enzymes, 11, 19, 26, 28, 36,
39, 40, 42, 60, 61, 83

F

fatigue, 3, 7, 9, 13, 1, 2, 5, 9,
12, 15, 17-20, 24, 26,
28, 54, 73, 74, 80, 81,
83, 105, 122-125,
131, 153-155
fear, 11, 6, 93, 117-119
fears, 11, 117-119
Fibromyalgia, 3, 7, 9, 13, 9,
12, 15, 18, 49, 52, 54,
55, 67, 73, 74, 77,
123, 124, 154, 155
fish oil, 54-58, 64, 67, 82
From Fatigued to Fantastic,
17, 61, 154
fruit, 2, 39, 83, 144

G

gas, 11, 2, 17, 21, 24, 59-61
Goldstein, Dr. Jay A., 25,
28, 29, 154
gratitude, 85, 86, 92

H

healing, 11, 9, 56, 61, 67,

76, 83, 87, 103, 105,
110, 113, 119, 153
healing from the heart, 87,
119
heart, 9, 8, 10-12, 24, 31, 33,
34, 38, 46-48, 56, 67,
85, 87-90, 92, 93,
106, 107, 113, 114,
119
homeopathics, 7, 51, 55, 67
humor, 11, 82, 86, 92, 95,
104, 105, 107, 109,
110, 114

I

immune system, 9, 6, 11,
19, 20, 28, 33, 42,
52-54, 67, 106, 154
insomnia, 11, 2, 4, 80, 83,
121, 122, 124, 125,
129-131
irritable bowel, 10, 11, 21,
59, 61

L

laughter, 11, 85, 90, 92,
104-110, 114
lymphasizing, 10, 67, 68,
70

M

malabsorption, 21
marker, 10, 11, 21, 61
microforms, 20, 21
microwaves, 42

N

necessary energy compo-
nents, 19, 26
neurotransmitters, 21, 25,
82, 106, 122, 126

O

optimism, 10, 65, 91-93
oxygenation, 52, 68

P

pain, 2, 9, 11, 12, 16-18, 25,
39, 46, 49, 52, 54, 55,
58-60, 63-69, 75, 80,
88, 92, 106, 115, 119,
122, 125, 131
pain management, 63, 65,
66, 75
panic attack, 25
parasites, 10, 11, 5, 11, 21,
52, 60, 61

pH balance, 9, 23
professional help, 7, 10, 73,
    79, 81
protein, 27, 32, 33, 35-37,
    70, 149, 151
Prozac, 3

R

raw food, 39, 42
raw foods, 39, 42, 62
results, 9, 18, 33, 45, 46, 66,
    100, 117, 124, 127,
    129
results of an alkaline diet,
    9, 46

S

Seven steps to eliminate
    stress, 89, 119
sleep, 3, 4, 64, 80, 121-131
Stoll, Dr. Andrew, 55, 56,
    58
stress, 11, 5-9, 12, 20, 60,
    61, 69, 87, 89, 90, 93,
    95, 97, 105-108, 119,
    126
success, 13, 46, 115, 123
success stories, 46
sugar, 19, 26, 35, 39, 42, 47,
    54, 61-64, 69, 83, 130

supplements, 9, 10, 7, 21,
    37, 45, 48, 51, 54, 57,
    66, 67, 76, 105, 129
support groups, 10, 18, 76,
    77
symptoms of depression,
    80

T

Tartaric acid test, 17
Teitelbaum, Dr. Jacob, 73,
    74, 75, 154
The China Study, 9, 31, 153
The pH Miracle, 12, 16, 155
The Yeast Connection, 18,
    61, 153, 154
thyroid, 21, 24
thyroid gland, 24

U

under active thyroid, 24

V

vegan, 11, 49, 135-139, 142,
    143, 145
vegan diet, 11
victim, 97, 98, 102
victim language, 102

W

water, 6, 12, 13, 36, 37, 43,
        49, 67, 69, 71, 104,
        111, 130, 134, 135,
        139, 141, 142, 144,
        146-148, 151, 152
whole foods, 33, 45
wormwood, 11, 52

Y

yeast, 9-11, 10, 15-18, 20-
        22, 35, 51, 52, 61, 75,
        83, 131, 153, 154
Young, 9, 4, 12, 13, 16, 20,
        21, 23, 24, 36, 43, 61,
        75, 76, 111, 155

A Note About the Author

Dr. Patty Butts has seven children, six step-children, and over 60 grandchildren. In addition to the extensive community, church, and professional service she has rendered, she still has found time to garden.

About the Type

The text of this book was set in Palatino Linotype. The fonts were originally designed by Hermann Zapf in 1948. The foundry version was cut in steel by August Rosenberger at the Stempel Foundry in Frankfurt. Zapf then adapted it for the Linotype machine. In photo and digital form, it has become the most widely used of all the neohumanist faces. It is popular among typographic professionals because in its authentic incarnations, Palatino is a superbly balanced, powerful and graceful contribution to typography.

Interior Designed by Mill Creek Press
Salt Lake City, Utah
Cover by Bill Witsberger
Salt Lake City, Utah
Printed and bound by BookSurge, LLC,
Charleston, South Carolina